Armenia

Armenia

BY MARTIN HINTZ

Enchantment of the World
Second Series

Children's Press®

A Division of Scholastic Inc.

NEW YORK TORONTO LONDON AUCKLAND SYDNEY
MEXICO CITY NEW DELHI HONG KONG
DANBURY, CONNECTICUT

Frontispiece: Singing Fountain, Republic Square, Yerevan

Consultant: Barlow Der Mugrdechian, Armenian Studies Program,
California State University, Fresno

Please note: All statistics are as up-to-date as possible at the time of publication.

Book production by Herman Adler Design

Library of Congress Cataloging-in-Publication Data

Hintz, Martin.
    Armenia / by Martin Hintz.
        p. cm. — (Enchantment of the world. Second series)
Summary: Describes the geography, plants and animals, history, economy, language,
religions, culture, sports, arts, and people of Armenia.
Includes bibliographical references and index.
        ISBN 0-516-24257-1
    1. Armenia (Republic)—History—Juvenile literature. 2. Armenia (Republic)—
        Geography—Juvenile literature. [1. Armenia (Republic).] I. Title. II. Series.
    DK685.6.H56 2004
    947.56—dc22   2003014669

Acknowledgments

Thanks to those who assisted with research on Enchantment of the World—*Armenia*. Whether through their own writings, suggestions, or reviews of this book as it progressed, their knowledge, creativity, and encouragement were immensely helpful.

Starting with H.F.B. Lynch, whose travels and studies on Armenia between 1893 and 1894 and in 1898 showed how curiosity leads to knowledge, nods of appreciation are necessary. Thanks to Ambassador Arman Kirakossian, Counselor Tigram Seyranian, and Second Secretary Noune Zastoukhova of the Armenian Embassy in Washington, D.C. Thanks also go to the Very Rev. Haigazoun Melkonian, Fr. Daron Stepanian, Jeff Davidian, and Hratch Tchilingirian. Also, thanks to reporters and inveterate travelers Matthew Karanian, Robert Kurkjian, Beth Potter, Levon Abrahamian, Nancy Sweezy, Hripsime Pikichian, and Kerop Bedoukian.

And there are more. Historians Ronald Grigor Suny, A.E. Redgate, and Vahan M. Kurkjian as well as photographers Sam Sweezy and Zaven Khachikyan. Dave Luhrssen presented helpful insights on his ancestral homeland. The congregants of Milwaukee's Saint John the Baptist Armenian Apostolic Church were generous with their warmth and hospitality.

And always thanks to the author's wife, Pam, who patiently listened to every marvelous detail about Armenia.

To Vanoush, Aghavni, Haigo, Vartanoush, Zareh, Rebecca, and all the other children who lost their lives during the Armenian Genocide, 1915–1918.

Contents

Cover photo:
Ruins of the twelfth-century Monastery of the Lance

Temple of the Sun

Young Armenians

The Cradle of Humankind

Armenia, the paradise land,
The cradle of humankind.
—ancient Armenian poem

GREAT CLOUDS OF SNOW AND HEAVY MIST ALWAYS SWIRL around the towering Caucasus Mountains of rugged Armenia. The narrow ledges and sheer cliffsides of this Near Eastern nation are home only to a few endangered mountain goats and sheep. But there are spirits up here. High atop the peaks, the ghosts of Armenia's past are alive and eager to sing their songs of bravery and love. The ghosts of kings and peasants, priests and warriors, children and elders feel the need to partake in today's Armenia. Their whispers dance like a wind-whipped blizzard. These mountains and this spirit world are proof of Armenia's courage in the face of generations of adversity.

Armenia does not dwell on the past, although reminders of its history are everywhere—in its churches, museums, cemeteries, folk traditions, literature, songs, and crafts. People lived in what is now Armenia before the dawn of civilization, during the Stone Age. The word *Armenia* was known 500 years before Christ was born. This region was located on the Silk Road, a pathway for trade that linked the Far East with Europe and Africa. Conquerors thundered through Armenia, some

Opposite: **The Caucasus Mountains include several peaks that reach heights of more than 16,404 feet (5,000 m).**

Zvartnots, a temple built in 641–661, was designed to impress all who viewed it. Today, all that remain are its ruins.

staying briefly, others staying for hundreds of years. Each group left something of its identity behind to be absorbed, used, and improved on by the locals.

The Armenians call themselves *Hye*, and the ancient name for their land is *Hayastan*. It is believed that these words came from the name of Haik, who started the Armenian family tree. Haik was a descendant of Noah, the man who saved all living creatures from drowning during the Great Flood, whose story is told in the Old Testament.

The Armenians are noted for creative expression whether in art, music, architecture, drama, or literature. Considered by scholars to be the first Christian nation, much of the country's marvelous art can be seen in the design of its ancient churches. Armenia's holy sites are sprinkled everywhere across the rugged landscape, ensuring that the memories of long ago are never forgotten. Beautifully illustrated, handwritten scriptures, lovingly-made sacred objects used in liturgies, and wonderfully uplifting hymns bring to life the ancient past and provide a bridge to worshipping today.

Armenia's secular world is also well known for its artistic accomplishments, whether with vibrant paintings hanging in public museums or by impressive outdoor sculptures prominently placed in city parks. Youngsters love visiting museums, especially the Children's Art Gallery of Yerevan, the country's capital, as well as going to films and other shows. Art and music schools are always packed with pupils excited to learn and to practice.

Music performed on traditional instruments remains an integral part of the country's social life. Weddings involve intricate dances to tunes handed down over the generations. Parents pass along their love of music to their youngsters, teaching them how to play and sing old songs. Yet Armenians also love modern jazz and rock music, just as do fans in other parts of the world.

When Armenia's soviet political system collapsed in 1991, the country became a republic. Young Armenia has contended

Today, Armenians look forward to national and economic stability.

with war, natural disasters, and economic challenges. However, in a short amount of time, Armenia has worked to develop an optimistic future. Armenia has been taking small steps to reach its goals of stability and prosperity.

Although there are many challenges facing Armenia's industries, the country's workers are highly respected. They are enthusiastic, skillfully producing many kinds of products. Transportation systems are constantly being improved in order to get goods out to ever-expanding worldwide markets. Roads are being built, bridges constructed, and airports expanded so that Armenia can ensure that its future remains bright. Businessmen and women eagerly showcase and sell what their country has to offer. More and more doors are opening in Europe, Asia, Africa and North America for Armenian goods.

The story of Armenia is not just one about a small country. It is a story of a people dispersed around the world, with large communities of Armenians living in the United States and Canada. Despite having to flee their homeland as desperate refugees, most Armenians living abroad have retained a strong belief in their national and personal identities. This fierce pride of country, church, and heritage has been passed down from generation to generation.

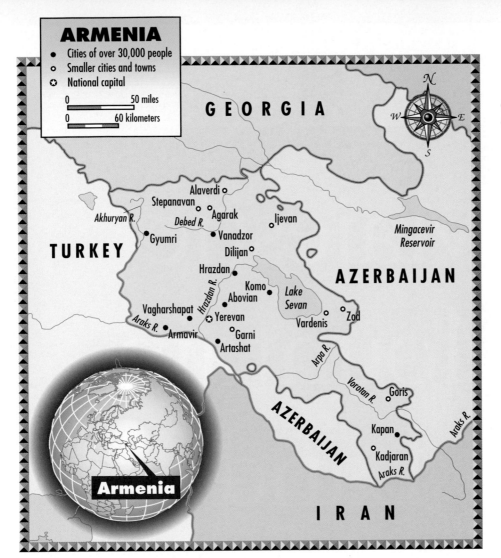

Geopolitical map
of Armenia

Today, some Armenians who have been living abroad are returning home to help rebuild their homeland. Others are contributing money to important causes that promote education or support business. Young Armenians all over the world join youth clubs, dance groups, and social organizations designed to keep their culture alive and vibrant. They are always welcome when they decide to return to their homeland. Armenia's spirits are waiting.

Majestic Mountain Land

MOUNTAINOUS ARMENIA IS SHAPED LIKE A TRIANGLE and is dominated by the snow-covered peaks of the Lesser Caucasus Mountains. These lofty crests run across the northern part of the country and then run southeast. A wide plateau slopes away from the mountains to the southwest and is the primary geographic mass in the center of Armenia.

Armenia's 779 miles (1,254 kilometers) of borders touch on four neighboring countries: Georgia to the north, Iran to the south, Turkey to the west, and Azerbaijan to the east.

Landlocked Armenia is slightly smaller than the U.S. state of Maryland and the European country of Belgium. It is the smallest of the republics that once made up the Soviet Union. Armenia covers a total of 11,505.8 square miles (29,800 square km).

Opposite: **Armenia is a place of mountains and rolling hills.**

Armenia's Mountains

Armenia's mountains are the stuff of history and legend. The entire country is high above sea level. The elevation of this jagged landscape averages between 3,300 feet (1,006 meters) and 8,250 feet (2,515 m), with the lowest point at 1,312 feet (400 m) above sea level. Mount Ararat remains the symbol of Armenia, although it has been under Turkish control since the 1921 Treaty of Moscow was signed between Russia and Turkey. In ancient times, this peak was within Armenian territory, and Armenians still have emotional ties to the

Mount Ararat is Armenia's sacred mountain and a source of inspiration for all Armenians.

mountain. Seen from the capital of Yerevan, Mount Ararat rears its rocky forehead over the dry, dusty plains and the sprawl of apartments. Mount Ararat is mysterious. It is believed to be the peak where Noah's ark finally settled after the Great Flood described in folklore and in Biblical verse. However, the honor of being the highest mountain in Armenia goes to an ancient volcano called Mount Aragats in the northwestern part of the country. This peak soars 13,418 feet (4,090 m) into the clouds.

Among the tallest mountains in Armenia is Kaputjukh, soaring 12,815 feet (3,906 m) in the Zangezur Chain of snow- and ice-covered ridges. Ajhdahak reaches 11,804 feet

Armenia's Geographical Features

Highest Elevation: Mount Aragats, 13,418 feet (4,090 m)

Lowest Elevation: Debed River, 1,312 feet (400 m) above sea level

Longest River: Araks, 568 miles (914 km)

Largest Lake: Sevan, 525 square miles (1,360 sq m)

Largest City: Yerevan, approximately 1.2 million residents

Average Precipitation: 8 to 31 inches (20 to 78 cm)

Average Temperatures: July, 71.6°F to 78.8°F (22°C to 26°C); January, 26.6°F to 14°F (−5°C to −10°C)

(3,598 m) in the Geghama Chain. In the Karabakh Chain, Mets Ishkhanasar towers 11,644 feet (3,549 m). The Vardenis Chain boasts of Mount Vardenis, which rises to 11,555 feet (3,522 m).

Armenia's rocky face consists of limestone, granite, and marble in addition to such exotic stones as perlite and pumice. The mountains are rich in minerals, including mercury, tungsten, gold, silver, copper, and tin. Small deposits of diamonds, turquoise, and emeralds also have been found in various parts of the country.

Trembling Earth

Earthquakes regularly shake Armenia because the country is located on top of shifting crustal plates of rock. Massive earthquakes in 1926 and 1988 (pictured) caused widespread destruction and huge economic loss. The latter earthquake killed approximately 25,000 people. The ancient city of Gyumri, located in northwest Armenia on the banks of the Akhuryan River, was destroyed in both earthquakes and was rebuilt each time. Help for the victims came from around the world. The Armenian government now encourages the construction of homes, offices, and factories that are less likely to collapse during earthquakes.

Beautiful Lake Sevan

In addition to its towering mountains, Armenia has another major geographic feature, Lake Sevan. This lake covers about 6 percent of the country's surface area, making it one of the largest mountain lakes in the world. The lake and its surrounding sand beaches are 6,232 feet (1,900 m) above sea level.

The famous Russian writer Maksim Gorky (1868–1936) called Lake Sevan a "piece of the sky that had descended to the earth among the mountains." Artists and photographers still delight in portraying its clean, clear water, whose coloring varies between a soft blue and a gentle turquoise. The water temperature remains about 64° Fahrenheit to 75°F (18° Celsius to 22°C) throughout the summer, making for a refreshing swim. Many vacationers from nearby Yerevan come here to escape the city's dust and heat. Besides taking a dip, they fish or explore the ancient monasteries that overlook the water.

Wetlands around Lake Sevan are part of Sevan National Park, which is managed by the Ministry of Nature Protection. Scientists from many countries study the numerous varieties of fish and birds living in the lake's coves and inlets.

Major rivers in Armenia include the Araks, which forms the border with Turkey and Iran. The only outlet for Lake Sevan is the Hrazdan River. Numerous hydroelectric plants along the riverbanks provide inexpensive electricity for Armenia's industries.

Lake Sevan, the largest lake of the Caucasus, is a stunning backdrop for the ninth-century church of Saint Arakelots.

A Dry Land

Droughts occur regularly in Armenia. They allow heavy winds to blow away the dry, thin, black- and chestnut-colored topsoil. The lack of rain is hard on crops, and

dark, thick clouds of swirling dirt sometimes make it difficult for people to see. The dust often seeps through cracks in doorways and windows and puts a thin layer of grime on tables, shelves, and chairs, no matter how often homes are cleaned. The arid semidesert near the Turkish border in the southeast is usually the hardest hit when rain fails to fall.

A severe drought in the year 2000 killed crops as rivers and irrigation canals ran dry. The lack of rain also affected livestock production, because cattle had a hard time finding fresh grass to eat, particularly in northern Armenia. Without feed, many farmers had to sell off their herds. This caused the price of livestock to drop because so many cows were being sold on the market.

Climate Zones

Within its hilly terrain, Armenia has several climate zones and four distinct seasons. Because of its elevation and location far inland, most of Armenia has a temperate climate and hot, dry summers with temperatures between 71.5°F and 96.8°F (22°C and 36°C). Armenia's winters can be very cold and snowy, with temperatures between 23°F and 14°F (−5°C and −10°C). Snow remains on the high mountains until late spring. The wind whips the ice and snow up there, creating frozen, tundra-like conditions. There is little humidity in summer or winter.

Winter in Yerevan

The country's temperate climate in the north and south is favorable for forest growth. Other large growths of various species of trees are found in some lower-lying districts, particularly in the southeast around Karabakh and Ijevan.

Conservation and Environmental Issues

Armenia faced numerous environmental challenges during the Soviet era, many of them man-made. Soil was polluted by toxic chemicals such as DDT, once used to wipe out insects

A Look at Armenian Cities

Vanadzor is Armenia's second-largest city. Its approximately 147,400 residents are primarily of Armenian heritage. This major railway center serves numerous chemical and textile factories. Vanadzor is located in northern Armenia at the junction of the Pambak, Tandzut, and Vanadzoriget rivers. The average temperature in January ranges between 20°F and 39°F (−6°C and 3°C). In July, the temperature is between 73°F and 96.8°F (23°C and 36°C). Because more than 70 percent of the city was destroyed by the 1988 earthquake, Vanadzor is still slowly rebuilding. Known as the City of Spas, Vanadzor attracts people from around the region to bathe in its rich mineral waters. It also has several universities and technical colleges.

Ancient tombs dating back three thousand years have been found near Vanadzor. Over the centuries, the city's strategic location made it a prize for the Persians, Tartars, Mongols, Turks, and Russians. It had many names over the years, including Gharakilisa and Kirovakan. Vanadzor was named a sister city of Pasadena, California, in 1991.

Gyumri is one of the oldest inhabited cities in the world, with its first historical record dating from the Argishti Dynasty in the seventh century B.C. The modern city, called Aleksandropol, dates its founding as 1837. Between 1924 and 1990, the city's name was changed to Leninakan, named for Vladimir Lenin, a communist revolutionary leader of the former Soviet Union. Today, Gyumri is Armenia's third-largest city and is home to 125,300 residents. Ninety-eight percent of the population is of Armenian heritage, but there are Russians, Greeks, and Kurds living there as well. The minimum temperature recorded in the winter is approximately 26°F (−3°C), and the maximum temperature recorded in the summer is 93°F (34°C). The city has several important archaeological sites dating from the Iron Age (750 B.C.–A.D. 42) as well as medieval churches and huge cemeteries holding the remains of victims from the 1988 earthquake that devastated much of the region.

Nuclear power is an important issue in Armenia. Although the EU wants the Metsamor power plant shut down, Armenia's minister of finance states that "we will not . . . until we provide the country with an alternative power source."

and now known to be very dangerous to many fish, birds, and insect species. Other pollutants from factory runoff contaminated the Razdan and Araks rivers. There were additional problems with industry. The Metsamor Nuclear Power Plant was said to operate without adequate safety precautions. There was always the danger of a radiation leak, especially during one of Armenia's many earthquakes. The European Union has demanded that the plant be shut down by 2005.

Drinking-water supplies are threatened by the draining of Lake Sevan, whose waters are being used as a source of hydro-electric power and for irrigation. However, natural mineral springs are found in the mountainous districts of Tavush and Lori, their bubbling waters full of calcium and other minerals.

Political problems have also created environmental crises. Armenia has had a lengthy conflict with neighboring Azerbaijan over control of the territory of Nagorno-Karabakh. The conflict is between the Armenian population of Nagorno-Karabakh and the rulers of Azerbaijan. Armenia supports what it says is its people's right to self-determination. However, Azerbaijan and its ally, Turkey, closed their borders, making it difficult for Armenia to receive oil and gas ship-ments for fuel. In the early days of the conflict, desperate Armenians had to scavenge for firewood. Thousands of trees were cut down and burned for heat and cooking fuel.

Modern Armenia has signed many international clean air and water agreements. The country wants to work with others to preserve its environment. As it matures as a nation, Armenia is cutting back on the dumping of factory waste and is curbing air pollution.

Plant Species in Danger

Because of the impact of humans and natural disasters such as drought and earthquakes, almost half the plant species grow-ing in Armenia faces some threat of environmental difficulty. At least thirty-five species are known to have become extinct over the past twenty-five years. Many others, including fifteen types of mushrooms, are threatened. Botanists, scientists who study plants, worry that plants such as the sweet flag bulrush, a valuable medicinal herb, and the Judas tree are endangered as more land is used for agriculture. Even the processing of sand for construction has endangered the small flowers found in the quarries.

The endangered Judas tree

Armenian shepherds keep a watchful eye over their flock. Overgrazing tends to harm plants and vegetation.

Draining wetlands further threatens a number of Armenia's water plants, such as the yellow water lily, the flowering rush, and the bogbean. Over the past few years, more than 49,400 acres (20,000 hectares) of marshland has been converted to farmland. The growing use of medicinal plants to treat illness also has caused problems. Plants such as the sweet flag bulrush, traditionally used to treat stomach and bowel problems, are being collected to be sold in markets abroad. Plucked or pulled by eager harvesters, they are not given enough time to regrow.

Overgrazing of grasslands by domestic sheep and cattle also contributes to the challenge of keeping native plants healthy and alive. Longtime industrial pollution of waterways is another serious problem. Under the Soviet regime, no one paid much attention to the environmental challenges caused by dumping toxic substances into rivers and lakes. It is hard for today's cash-poor Armenia to clean up these environmental problems. But a growing number of its citizens, led by the scientific community, is working hard to repair what problems they can.

Blossoms
and Bears

ARMENIA HAS A WIDE VARIETY OF FLOWERS BECAUSE of its unique geographic position. Snow-capped mountains are only a few hours away from subtropical valleys. The outer reaches of Armenia are relatively undisturbed. Therefore, a range of wildflowers, natural grasses, trees, and shrubs carpet the landscape. This blend of climate and geography contributes to the country's botanical diversity. Overall, 108 species of plants unique to Armenia have been counted. There is evidence that the trees existing today also existed in antiquity, even though the climate changed over the centuries. Fossil remains have been found of pine, walnut, spruce, and cedar. Several varieties of fungi and ferns, as well as the yew and Oriental beech, are known to be very ancient. Armenian scholars studied these plants as early as the fifteenth century. Their written observations are helpful today to botanists, those who study plant life.

Most of the country's thickest forests are located in the northeastern and southeastern regions. Wide stretches of grassy steppe, featuring a prairie-like landscape, are present to the north of Armenia's

Opposite: **Yellow wild-flowers thrive in Armenia's mountainous landscape.**

Environmental groups hope that Armenia's forests will expand by 25 percent by the year 2059.

Armenia's mountainous nature features diverse landscapes, such as this alpine meadow.

southwestern desert zone. Wormwood and other brushy plants grow in the semidesert. Alpine meadows can be found in the mountain foothills, primarily in central Armenia. The country's various soils affect what vegetation grows where, with the thickest, most fertile earth found in the deep valleys. The coarsest growth is found in the mountains.

Mid-June to mid-July is the best time for viewing such floral beauties as wild geraniums, gladiolus, and delphinium. Artists love the palette of green water lilies around the lakes near Stepanavan. Specialists help visitors seek out the best places to observe all these vibrant, growing things. Nora Gabrielian, a professor at the Armenian Botanical Society, is considered one of her country's most renowned botanical specialists. Whenever she can take time from her research at the society, Gabrielian guides international groups wanting to study Armenia's plant life. She takes scientists from Japan, Canada, and other countries on flower-seeking treks from the plateaus of Mount Aragats to Armenia's dry, low-lying valleys.

Gladiolus (left) and delphinium (right) thrive during Armenia's warm summers.

Armenia's variety of furry, scaly, and feathered animal life ranges from the small to the large. The list of local creatures found only in Armenia includes a rare, long-eared desert hedgehog. The tiny animal sometimes scoots its way into vineyards and orchards in search of insects, lizards, and small rodents to eat. In Armenia, scientists have recorded approximately seventeen thousand invertebrates, or animals without backbones, of which 90 percent are insects. Of these, more than three hundred are considered to be rare or declining because of such natural disasters as drought. In addition, the country's ongoing economic crisis results in overhunting certain areas for food. Animals also face problems resulting from the lack of effective environmental rules.

Six species are almost extinct, including a rare mountain sheep, the mouflon, which lives on cliffs and high plateaus in central and southern Armenia's Khosrov reservation. Once numerous, only a few hundred of the great, horned beasts can be spotted today, leaping from ledge to ledge 2,624 to 12,795 feet (800 to 3,900 m) above sea level.

The rare mouflon can be found on the steep and rocky cliffs of Armenia.

Brown bears wander through the relatively unpopulated regions of southeastern Armenia, sometimes climbing as far as the higher slopes of the mountains. The bears move heavily along looking for grubs and berries to eat. They live in forests, stopping in caves and ravines when they want to sleep. The clearing of trees has reduced the size of safe areas where the bears can roam. By the early 2000s, scientists counted only 150 of these creatures in Armenia. Other animals that may

Brown bears are losing their homes due to the lack of forestland in Armenia.

European otters (right) are becoming uncommon creatures in Armenia, while the striped hyena (below) cannot be found at all.

soon disappear are the wild goat, the marbled polecat, and the European otter. The striped hyena and the Caucasian birch mouse are probably already extinct because no sign of them has been noted in the past few years.

A common reptile found among Armenia's rocky slopes is the skink.

Life Above and Below the Water

Armenia has thirty-one different species of fish swimming in its waters. Lake Sevan is home to the prized *ishkhan* (prince) trout, which is considered a delicacy. White bream and catfish are also found in most of the country's waterways. Yet once again, human activity is threatening the watery habitat where these fish swim and spawn, or reproduce. Overfishing and pollution are the two biggest environmental challenges to preserving Armenia's fish population.

Armenia's rocky landscape is home to the rare skink and rock and white-bellied lizards. An amphibian, the Syrian

An Armenian viper suns itself on warm stones.

spadefoot toad, can also be counted among the country's critters. Added to the list of Armenian slithery creatures are the Caucasian rat snake and the Armenian viper.

The Armenian gull is considered to be the only bird truly native to Armenia. The large gull lives in the Lake Sevan basin and along several of Armenia's rivers. The white-winged scoter,

The Armenian gull nests among the wetlands of Lake Sevan and Armenia's rivers.

which is a species of duck, and the boreal owl are two other birds found primarily in Armenia and its neighboring nations. Lake Lichk is an important breeding site for other species of ducks, as well as for grebes and coots. The great white pelican nests alongside some of Armenia's lakes. These pelicans once called Lake Sevan their home, but most left when the water level started dropping due to hydroelectric and irrigation projects.

White pelicans are a common sight along rivers in Armenia.

National Zoo

Armenia's compact national zoo is located in the hills east of Yerevan. It is open from May to September. Families take a bus from Republic Square in downtown Yerevan to the pleasant, tree-shrouded park. There they can see mountain sheep and lions in their natural settings. Interested in their country's natural history, Armenians from around the world have contributed to the zoo's upkeep and expansion.

The Armenia Tree Project, promoted by the Armenian Assembly of America, was founded in 1993 to fund reforestation of the land. Since that time, the group has planted more than 300,000 trees and has opened two tree nurseries. It also launched fruit-drying and distribution businesses for poverty-stricken villages and has hired hundreds of Armenians to care for damaged forests. For its efforts, the project was awarded the prestigious National Arbor Day Foundation Project Award in 2002.

This replanting of trees is greatly appreciated in Armenia for many reasons, among which is the production of fruit, nuts, and seeds for people to include in their diets. Trees also provide feed for animals. In addition, wood is a renewable source of fuel for a country that has long depended on scarce and expensive foreign oil and gas. Lumber and pulp can be used for construction and the making of paper products. Trees also prevent soil erosion and clean the air.

Despite its environmental challenges, Armenia would like to see ecotourism increase in the countryside. This would encourage locals to take better care of their land. In response, the government has set aside protected territories that occupy 10 percent of its total land. These protected areas include Sevan National Park, five state preserves (Khosrov, Dilijan, Shikahogh, Sevlid, and Rebuni), and twenty-two state reservations still under development. The World Bank is helping Armenia plan ecotourism programs in the provinces of Tavush and Geghark'unik'.

This dramatic waterfall is found in Armenia's Jermuk nature preserve.

Dipping into the Past

In Armenia, graveyards provide researchers with a window to the past.

Humans have lived in what is today's Armenia for thousands of years. It is estimated that the first permanent agricultural settlement in Armenia was established near Lake Van around 6000 B.C. Archaeologists believe that the original, or "proto," Armenians who spoke the roots of today's Armenian language came here from the west to mingle with the existing Hurrian civilization. The first formal archaeological dig in Armenia, which took place in 1876, uncovered seventy-six prehistoric graves near Dilijan. Fragments of bone, tools, and other artifacts were uncovered, giving scientists clues about life in those long-ago days. Over the years, scientists have discovered hundreds of other burial sites around the towns of Alaverdi and Akhtala. Some of these sites are estimated to be ten thousand years old. By studying stone, iron, bronze, and clay artifacts found in the graves, researchers can trace the changes in daily life in Armenia through the ages.

Opposite: **The thirteenth-century illustration of *The Birthday Feast of Nubien, King of Armenia.***

What's in a Name?

Historians and scholars say that the name of Armenia was first written in an inscription by the Persian king Darius I in 521 B.C. The inscription, carved in three languages on a cliffside near the city of Kermanshah, describes this ancient country. The name *Armina* was used in the Persian, *Harminia* in the Elamic, and *Urashtu* in the Babylonian language. Hundreds of years ago, Greek historians referred to the people in Armenia as *Armenians*, a term derived from the name of the Armen tribe.

This relief depicts Persian guards with spears and shields. The Persians ruled Armenia for many centuries.

Assyrians, Persians, and Greeks
680 B.C. – A.D. 114

▨ Assyrian Empire, 680 B.C.	—— Roman Empire, ca. A.D. 114
▨ Persian Empire, ca. 530 B.C.	⋯⋯ Modern-day Armenia
—— Empire of Alexander, 323 B.C.	

Treasured Location

Because of its location, Armenia is one of the most trampled-over countries in the world. Its position on the trade routes between Asia and Europe made it a valuable prize. Despite this challenge to their cultural identity, the Armenians successfully absorbed invading new-comers, who often settled down and intermarried with the locals. The Persians, who came from what is now the country of Iran, gave the Armenians some control over their own territory between the ninth and sixth centuries B.C. As long as the Armenians supplied the Persian court with fine horses and paid their taxes, they were left alone.

Peace never lasted long, however. Alexander the Great, a famous Macedonian general, defeated the Persians in 331 B.C. but bypassed Armenia while moving east. In approximately 190 B.C., the Romans replaced the Greeks as the rulers of the empire Alexander had created. To help them govern their far-flung empire, the Romans installed Armenians as local rulers. One was Artaxias, a powerful nobleman who lay the foundation for an Armenian kingdom, although it was still under the watchful eye of the Roman Empire.

Armenia became part of the vast Roman Empire around 190 B.C.

Garni, Summer Home of Kings

Located 22 miles (35 km) south of Yerevan is the village of Garni, famous for its pagan Temple of the Sun. The building dates from the first century B.C. and was used as late as A.D. 330. The ruins of the structure are located inside a fortress used as the summer home of Armenia's early kings. The complex was damaged during an earthquake in 1679 and was restored in the 1970s. In medieval Armenia, Garni became known as a monastic center and still has many churches that draw tourists.

One of the greatest figures of the time was Tigranes II (often called Tigran the Great), the grandson of Artaxias. Under his administration, Armenia became one of the most powerful states in the southwestern corner of Asia. During Tigranes's reign, from 95 to 55 B.C., Greater Armenia stretched through Turkey, Azerbaijan, Georgia, Iran, Syria, and Iraq. Tigranes II was instrumental in uniting the ancient lands of North Syria, Mesopotamia, Cilicia, and Phoenicia. Yet the Romans never totally gave up their authority. In A.D. 113, they brought Armenia back under their total control and kept a close watch on all Armenian political activity.

Gregory the Illuminator, Apostle to Armenia, spread Christianity throughout Armenia and was founder of the Armenian church.

Tiridates III (A.D. 238–314) was placed on the Armenian throne in A.D. 259. Gregory the Illuminator, a notable Armenian saint, converted Tiridates and most of his followers to Christianity in approximately A.D. 301. Subsequently, Armenia was considered the first officially Christian nation. In 314, Tiridates was killed while hunting, and Armenia was divided into Byzantine Armenia and Persian Armenia.

Land of Ancient Religions

The Persians tried to get the Christian Armenians to convert to Zoroastrianism so they could exert

more control over their subjects. This was a very ancient, mystical religion that rejected the idea of the existence of multiple gods and concentrated on the spirit of good, Ahura Mazda, overcoming evil, Ahriman. However, the Armenians refused to give up their faith and revolted against Persian rule under the leadership of Vartan (or Vardan) Mamikonian. He was a noted general of Armenian heritage who had served bravely in the Persian army. His mother was a descendent of Gregory the Illuminator.

Mamikonian refused to follow his orders from the Persians and turn on his fellow Armenians. He organized a force to confront the Persians, whose huge army included trained elephants that carried archers. The two sides clashed in the fierce,

Above left: **A monument to Vartan Mamikonian, commander-in-chief who led the Armenians to battle the Persians in A.D. 451.**

Above right: **The Persian army went into battle on horses and elephants.**

one-day battle of Avarair in A.D. 451, in which Mamikonian was killed. However, the Persians also lost thousands of their troops and eventually decided to grant the Armenians their religious and political freedom. The Armenian church canonized Vartan, making him a saint.

Decades of relative calm followed. Leaders of the Christian clergy and the Armenian *nakharars* (princes) played instrumental roles in helping hold Armenia together. However, Muslims, followers of the prophet Muhammad, stormed north out of Arabia around A.D. 600. Muhammad (570–632) was born in the Arabian city of Mecca, now one of the world's most holy sites. Rejecting the many gods worshipped at the time, Muhammad founded Islam, in which one god, Allah, is worshipped.

While spreading Islam, the Muslims quickly conquered Persia and Armenia by 640. Again, the Armenians were persecuted for their faith and fiercely resisted the invaders. They waged a guerrilla-style war for almost one hundred years, an ongoing conflict in which Armenian fighters ambushed Muslim troops from the safety of the mountains. By the 800s, the battle-weary Muslims were ready to allow the Armenians some independence. They recognized Ashot I as the king of Armenia in 885 after he soundly defeated one of the Muslim armies. Under Ashot's rule, there was a long period of peace that allowed Armenian poetry and literature to flourish.

Cradle of War

Armenia was again threatened and eventually conquered in 1071 by the Seljuk Turks, who had taken control of the crumbling

Byzantine Empire. In 1088, an independent Armenian principality called Lesser Armenia was set up in the district of Cilicia. The Turks were in turn attacked by the Mongols, whose armies swept in from the east in 1240. During these wars, tens of thousands of Armenians fled their ancestral homelands and dispersed throughout southwest Asia and the Middle East. A group of Armenian princes spent much of their time fighting each other rather than keeping invaders away. With all the internal feuding, the kingdom of Lesser Armenia barely lasted until 1375.

War continued to wash over Armenia. Most powerful of the next wave of invaders were the Ottoman Turks. In the 1400s, they defeated the Seljuks.

Ottoman, Russian, and Persian Territories 1636–1828

☐ Russian Empire, 1795	— Boundary established by Peace of Zuhab, 1639
▨ Added to Russian Empire by 1828	⋯⋯ Modern-day Armenia

Map shows boundaries of 1828.

The Ottomans had one of the most powerful civilizations of its time. Their expansion built an empire that established Islamic culture and tradition.

Dipping into the Past **45**

Capture of Yerevan Fortress,
painted by M. Sedrakyan,
shows the historical libera-
tion of Yerevan by Russian
troops.

Armenia continued to be a pawn in these power struggles. In the 1600s, the Armenians were caught up in wars between the Ottomans and the Persians. In 1639, Armenia was split between these opponents, the west remaining with the Ottomans and the east going to the Persians. Amid the chaos, the Armenians looked outward for help. They hoped that the increasingly powerful Russian Empire would eventually come to their rescue. Under the reign of Catherine the Great between 1762 and 1796, the Russians expanded their control southward and seized territory in Armenia. By 1813, they had taken over neighboring Georgia, Karabakh, and most of Azerbaijan. In 1828, Armenian territories around Yerevan fell to the Russians. Unlike the many Muslim empires that had overrun Armenia, the Russians were Christians who supported the Armenian church. Many Armenians in Ottoman-held areas subsequently migrated to the Russian-dominated districts, where they felt safer. A large number of Armenians also went to the United States and Canada.

By the end of the 1800s, European nations were voicing their objections to the poor treatment of Armenians still living under brutal Ottoman rule. Their concerns were ignored, however, and there were widespread massacres of Armenians by the Ottoman sultan Abdul Hamid II between 1894 and 1896.

Worried that the Armenians would eventually seek independence, the once-friendly Russians, under the rule of Czar Nicholas II, outlawed Armenian schools and closed libraries. The Russians even occupied Armenian churches and seized land owned by monasteries. After an armed rebellion, the Armenians finally retrieved their property in 1905.

Abdul Hamid II was called "The Great Assassin" due to his treatment of Armenians.

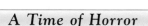

A Time of Horror

Faced with growing international tensions that eventually led to World War I, Europe forgot about the situation in Armenia. In World War I (1914–1918), Britain, France, Russia, and the

Armenian refugees in their desert camp

United States fought against Germany and Turkey. The Muslim Turks feared that the Christian Armenians in their territory would rise up and fight against them. Subsequently, beginning on April 24, 1915, they deported hundreds of thousands of Armenians to the barren Syrian Desert without food or water. Many refugees died or were killed along the

The Armenian Horror Story Retold

The horror of the Armenian genocide has been the central theme of many Armenian scholarly works, novels, films, and poems, which keep alive the memory of pain and suffering. Kerop Bedoukian was only nine years old when he was forced to leave his home after his father was arrested and never seen again. As an adult living in Canada, Bedoukian wrote a book called *Some of Us Survived*. It tells a small part of the nightmare through a child's eyes. *Ararat*, a gripping movie released in 2002 by award-winning Canadian-Armenian producer Atom Egoyan, also tells the terrible story.

way. Armenian villages were burned and their inhabitants murdered in what the Armenians today call the genocide, or destruction, of their race. It is estimated that more than 1.5 million people died during this terrible time.

Before the war ended, the Russian imperial government was so weak that it collapsed. The czar abdicated, or stepped down from power. He was then imprisoned and murdered along with his family. Communists, people who supported an economy in which the government controls the means of production so that wealth can be distributed equally, took power and initially allowed some outlying areas of the old Russian Empire to organize their own governments. A group of Armenian revolutionaries, including the Dashnaks, formed an Armenian Republic in 1918. It was the first time in centuries that the Armenians had full control over their own lands, although the republic was only one-tenth the size of historic Armenia.

Freedom did not last long. In November of 1920, Armenia, Azerbaijan, and Georgia were brought under the Soviet Union's political umbrella. They were united as the Transcaucasian Soviet Federated Socialist Republic in 1922. The dreams of an independent Armenia were once again dead. Yet under the repressive communist regime, Armenia was transformed into a Western-style nation. Factories, dams, and irrigation works were constructed. Then, as always in this region, political winds changed. In 1936, Armenia, Azerbaijan, and Georgia were again separated, becoming individual republics of the Soviet Union.

Terrors of War

During World War II (1939–1945), Armenia was spared the destruction that swept much of the rest of the Soviet Union. The German armies that invaded the Soviet Union never got beyond the Caucasus Mountains. Armenian industry and agriculture continued to aid the Allied cause, which eventually defeated the Axis powers. However, it is estimated that 300,000 Armenians died during the conflict. After the war, attention was again focused on increasing Armenia's industrial output. Armenians were still not free, however. Farmers could not own their land and instead worked on collective farms owned by the state. Politics were closely controlled, and the Armenians' dreams of independence were discouraged by threats and outright force.

Although more than half the world's 6.3 million Armenians were dispersed outside its borders by this time, Soviet Armenia still had the largest concentration of Armenians in the world. By the 1960s, a complex struggle emerged between the conservative communists and Armenians seeking a greater voice in their own affairs.

People stand around the eternal flame that burns as part of a monument to the fallen victims of the Armenian genocide.

On April 24, 1965, thousand of residents of Yerevan, the capital of Soviet Armenia, demonstrated during a fiftieth anniversary commemoration of the Ottoman massacres. Soviet troops attempted to restore order. To halt any more turmoil, the Soviet government agreed to build several memorials to the fallen Armenians of 1915. Inspired by this action, Armenian artists and musicians began speaking out in praise of *mer hairenik* ("our fatherland"). Several underground separatist organizations were formed. One group was blamed for setting off a bomb that killed seven people in the Moscow subway. But most Armenians preferred to preserve their culture through peaceful actions. They encouraged the use of the Armenian language and customs, especially in Soviet republics outside Armenia.

Mikhail Gorbachev, who took charge of the Soviet Union in 1985, allowed people more freedom to discuss issues. Armenian nationalists took advantage of this new openness, which was called *glasnost* in the Russian language. Christian Armenians living in the Nagorno-Karabakh enclave of Muslim-ruled Azerbaijan voted to be free in 1988. In 1992, however, the rulers of Azerbaijan launched an attack on the people of Nagorno-Karabakh. Thousands were killed by the time a cease-fire was agreed on in May 1994.

After it gained its independence when the Soviet Union dissolved in 1991, Armenia's road to parliamentary democracy

Rubble remains from an Azerbaijani attack on Nagorno-Karabakh.

was rocky. No one was quite sure how this new system would work. Initially, Armenia adopted a system set up by its Soviet-style 1978 constitution. Under the old system, the chief executive was the chairman of Armenia's Supreme Soviet, the primary legislative body of the republic, who gave all the orders. However, no one wanted an old-style legislature that would simply do whatever the central government demanded.

In 1990, Levon Ter-Petrossian was elected as the leader of post-Soviet Armenia. Beginning in 1991, he secured special executive powers to deal with his country's political chaos and the war with Azerbaijan. Ter-Petrossian privatized much of the economy, which allowed private ownership of land and industry, and tried to resolve the fighting with Azerbaijan over the breakaway district of Karabakh. He also attempted to bring stability to the Armenian government. In 1992, the United States became the first foreign country to open an embassy in the Republic of Armenia, and the country joined the United Nations.

Between 1992 and 1994, Armenians continued to argue over whether to support a strong executive or a strong legislative branch of government. Many of these issues were resolved on July 5, 1995, when Armenian citizens voted in favor of a new constitution that guaranteed their civil rights and created a more democratic system of government.

President Re-elected

Voters re-elected President Ter-Petrossian in 1996, but he was forced to step down from his position in 1998. He had lost his

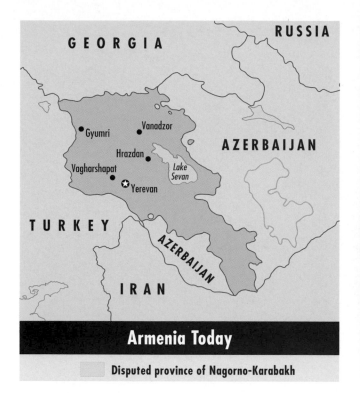

Armenia Today

Disputed province of Nagorno-Karabakh

Above: **President of Armenia, Robert Kocharian**

support when he argued that compromise was necessary to resolve the Nagorno-Karabakh conflict. Prime Minister Robert Kocharian won the following presidential election in 1998. He quickly met with the president of Azerbaijan to end the fighting. New peace talks held in October of that year were rejected by Azerbaijan because they did not guarantee the country's territorial integrity.

When the Soviet Union dissolved at the end of 1991, Armenia and its neighbors regained their independence. However, they needed immediate economic, military, and political help. Subsequently, Armenia joined the Commonwealth of Independent States, a confederation that united eleven of the fifteen former Soviet republics. Seeking a powerful friend, Armenia also turned to Russia, the strongest of

Three Soviet soldiers stand alongside a tank in Yerevan after Armenia turns to Russia for aid.

the former Soviet republics. Russia attempted to resolve the disputes between Armenia and Azerbaijan, but was largely unsuccessful. Assistance also came from farther away. The United States and the countries of the European Union sent much humanitarian and economic aid to Armenia between 1991 and 1994.

Unfriendly Neighbors

Armenia's relations with nearby countries have often been cool. Turkey blockaded Armenia during its war with Azerbaijan and accused Armenia of supporting rebelling

Kurds in their country. Turkey also denied responsibility for the 1915 massacres of Armenians, blaming the atrocity on the old Ottoman Empire. Because of its mistrust of Turkey, Armenia decided to approve another security treaty with Russia, which also was seeking to block Turkey's growing influence around the Black Sea and in the Caucasus Mountains.

Armenia struggles for stability despite a growing appreciation of the democratic process through elections. Five gunmen burst into Armenia's National Assembly on October 27, 1999, and killed Prime Minister Vazgen Sarksyan and seven other people. Many other people in the building were wounded and taken hostage. Soon after the attack, the rebels gave themselves up.

This photo of Armenia's prime minister, Vazgen Sarksyan, was taken three months prior to his assassination.

The attack undermined the relationship between President Kocharian and the rest of the government, which was backed by the National Assembly. Armenian politics stalled as the two sides struggled for power. Kocharian remained in office while the successor government, led by Sarksyan's brother Aram, was dismissed after six months. Andranik Markarian, a leader of the Republican Party, then became prime minister.

As evidenced by its turbulent history, Armenia still has a long, slow path to walk toward peace. Yet most of its citizens remain eager to reach that goal.

A New Look at Government

ARMENIA'S CONSTITUTION WAS ADOPTED AFTER BEING accepted in a nationwide vote on July 5, 1995. The constitution established a legal system based on civil law. Under Article Two of the Armenian constitution, governmental power resides with the people. They exercise their rights by choosing leaders through free elections and by voting on issues. State and local governments and public officials receive their authority through the constitution. The constitution also protects human rights and freedoms in accordance with

Opposite: **Demonstrators take to the streets of Yerevan, calling for new elections and a new constitution for Armenia.**

The Armenian Flag and Coat of Arms

The flag of the Republic of Armenia consists of three horizontal stripes of red, blue, and gold. The design was confirmed on August 24, 1990, and is identical to Armenia's first state flag, which flew from 1918 to 1921. Red represents the blood shed by Armenians who were fighting for their country, religion, and independence. Blue represents the country's sky, rivers, and lakes. Orange represents the country's resources.

The country's coat of arms has a shield in its center that includes a representation of Mount Ararat topped by Noah's ark. Within the shield are symbols of the four historical kingdoms of Armenia. The shield is held by a lion and an eagle (symbolizing wisdom, pride, and patience), along with a sword (symbolizing national strength), a feather pen (symbolizing intellectual and cultural heritage), a sheaf of wheat (symbolizing the hardworking people), a broken chain (symbolizing freedom), and a tricolor ribbon (symbolizing the flag). The contemporary coat of arms is based on one used by the first Republic of Armenia. It was originally designed by the architect Aleksandr Tamanyan and the painter Hagop Kojoyan.

international law. It safeguards individuals' property rights and takes a strong stand on protecting the environment. The constitution can be amended by a vote sought by the president of the republic or by the National Assembly.

The constitution set up a parliamentary democracy. Under this system, Armenia has a strong executive branch headed by a president, who is the chief of state. The president is elected

The First President of the Republic of Armenia

Levon Ter-Petrossian was born on January 9, 1945, in Aleppo, Syria, and immigrated to Armenia with his family in 1946. He graduated from the Oriental Studies Department of Yerevan State University in 1968 and then completed graduate studies at the Leningrad Oriental Studies Institute in 1971. In 1987, he received his doctorate before going to work as a researcher at the Literature Institute of Armenia.

Ter-Petrossian has written numerous scientific articles in Armenian, Russian, and French. He belongs to the Armenian Writers' Union, the French Asian Society, and many other educational and literary groups. He became active in politics in the 1960s, belonging to the Armenian Committee of the Karabakh movement. Ter-Petrossian was arrested for his work with this organization. After he was freed from jail, he was elected to the board of the Armenian National Movement and held several positions there. In 1989, he was elected to the Supreme Soviet, the parliament of the Armenian Soviet Socialist Republic. Re-elected in 1990, Ter-Petrossian became the Supreme Soviet's general chairman. He was elected as the first president of

the Republic of Armenia on October 16, 1991, and was re-elected in 1996. He resigned in February of 1998.

by popular vote for a five-year term. He can serve only two consecutive terms. A candidate must be at least thirty-five years old and a citizen who has been living in the republic for the preceding ten years. The president is elected by receiving more than half the number of eligible votes that are cast. If more than two candidates seek office, there is a runoff election between the two who received the most votes. Since March 30, 1998, the president of Armenia has been Robert Kocharian, who was elected to a second term in the spring of 2003.

The president is helped by a twenty-one-member cabinet that includes ministries of finance and justice. The candidates for positions in the ministries are suggested by a prime minister who is appointed by the president. The prime minister acts as the head of the government and handles the day-to-day running of Armenia. Government decisions are signed off on by the prime minister and approved by the president. The executive branch does not work alone. It must have its agenda, policies, and budget approved by the National Assembly.

In addition to running the country, the government is responsible for maintaining public order, ensuring the country's defense, and implementing state policies in science, education, culture, health, social security, and environmental protection.

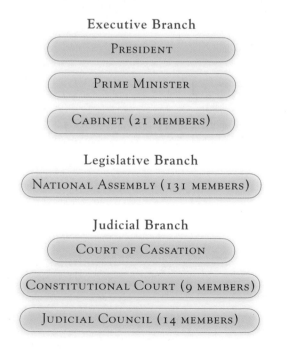

NATIONAL GOVERNMENT OF ARMENIA

Executive Branch

PRESIDENT

PRIME MINISTER

CABINET (21 MEMBERS)

Legislative Branch

NATIONAL ASSEMBLY (131 MEMBERS)

Judicial Branch

COURT OF CASSATION

CONSTITUTIONAL COURT (9 MEMBERS)

JUDICIAL COUNCIL (14 MEMBERS)

Within the National Assembly building, Armenia's members of parliament hold legislative sessions.

Armenia's Unicameral Assembly

The legislative branch of government is made up of a unicameral (one-house) National Assembly, or parliament. There are 131 seats, and members serve four-year terms. Seventy-five representatives are elected from small voting districts that are each allowed to have one member. The remaining fifty-six are elected members from larger districts that are allowed more members. The members, who are called deputies, select an assembly chairman. Until the chairman is chosen, meetings are chaired by the oldest deputy.

The National Assembly holds regular sessions between early February and mid-June and from mid-September to mid-December. Extra sessions can be called by the president of the republic, the president of the assembly, or one-third of the deputies. Anyone who is at least twenty-five years old, has been a citizen, and has lived in Armenia for the preceding five years may be elected to the National Assembly. Elections are held sixty days prior to the expiration, or ending, of the term of the existing assembly. Armenians love politics. They can vote when they reach eighteen years of age, a responsibility taken very seriously. All voting is secret.

There is a joke that if two Armenians get together to talk about how their country is governed, they will form three political parties. Many parties organized and disbanded in Armenia's first ten years of independence. These groups usually followed one popular leader or advocated a single issue. Others were formed more than a century ago and were active in the Armenian government from 1918 to 1921. Several of these parties are still strong in Armenian communities outside the country. A few returned to their homeland and have tried to re-establish themselves in the new Armenia.

Armenians are eligible to vote when they turn eighteen. This woman casts her ballot for president in the 2003 elections.

Multi-Party System

The existence of a multi-party system is guaranteed by the Armenian constitution. The Republican Party was the largest party in the National Assembly during the early 2000s. Others with elected representatives included the People's Party of Armenia and the Stability Group, which was made up of independent deputies who formed their own voting block. Others were the Armenian Revolutionary Federation (the Dashnaks) and the Law and Unity Party. Among those vigorously campaigning to win seats are the Armenian Communist Party and the Christian Democratic Union.

Country Justice

The Armenian judicial branch consists of the Court of Cassation, the Constitutional Court, and the Judicial Council. The duty of the Court of Cassation is to review other courts' verdicts and rulings after appeals by the Office of the Chief Prosecutor or by lawyers who are registered to practice at the court. The chief justice is nominated by the president and is elected by winning a simple majority of the vote in the National Assembly. The court includes a three-member criminal chamber; a three-member civil chamber that oversees cases that are not criminal; and an eleven-member presidium, or administrative committee, that is responsible for conducting final reviews of the court's actions. The Constitutional Court, which was established in 1995, has nine members. Five are appointed by the National Assembly and four by the president of the republic. Judges who serve in the Constitutional

Court can hold office until age seventy. This court rules on the constitutionality of laws, presidential decrees, and international agreements. It also has the final say on choosing a winner if there is a disputed election.

The president of the republic presides over the Judicial Council, as well as the minister of justice and the prosecutor general serving as its deputy heads. The fourteen members of the council are appointed by the president for a period of five years. They include two legal scholars, nine judges, and three prosecutors. The council is responsible for recommending the appointments of judges and prosecutors, as well as for taking disciplinary action against judges convicted of wrongdoing. The Office of the Prosecutor General oversees investigations, brings actions in court on behalf of the state, and carries out the verdicts and decisions of the courts.

Armenian soldiers stand at attention.

Guarding the Nation

The Armenian military consists of an army, an air force, and security forces made up of internal and border troops. Even after the Soviet Union collapsed, Armenia's national security still depended heavily on Russian support. When Armenia created its new army in 1992, many of the officers had served previously in the Soviet army or were trained in its military schools. Currently, two Russian divisions are based in Armenia and are under Armenian control. Armenians are drafted into the military at age eighteen, although deferments are granted to those who enter graduate school.

Armenia's local government consists of eleven administrative divisions, or provinces, called *marzer*. A single province is called a *marz*. The *marzer* include Aragatsotn, Ararat, Armavir, Geghark'unik', Kotaik, Lori, Shirak, Syunik, Tavush, and Vayots Dzor. Yerevan has its own special status as the capital. Each of the districts is governed on the local level by a council of elders, composed of five to fifteen members and a district administrator called a governor, who is aided by a staff. Each *marzhed* (governor) is appointed by the national government, while elected council members hold three-year terms. Cities and villages have mayors. The elder's council determines and implements the district's budget and levies taxes. Upon the recommendation of the prime minister, the president appoints the mayor of Yerevan.

Friends Around the World

Armenia belongs to numerous international organizations, such as the law-enforcement group Interpol. It joined the United Nations in 1992. Armenia has embassies around the world, including ones in the United States and Canada. There is also a consular office in Los Angeles. Many countries also have ambassadors in Armenia.

Armenia's National Anthem

The words to the national anthem, "Our Fatherland," were written by the famous Armenian poet and patriot Mikayel Ghazari Nalbandian (1829–1866), and the music was written by Barsegh Kanachyan (1885–1967). The current anthem, adopted on July 1, 1991, is a modified version of the earlier work that adds lyrics about the original anthem of freedom and independence of the country. To the fiercely proud Armenian people, this anthem honors their ancestors who fought to preserve their heritage.

Mer Hairenik

Mer Hairenik, azad angakh,
Vor abrel eh tareh tar
Ir vor tika art ganchoom eh
Azad, angakh haiasdan.
(repeat previous two lines)

Aha yeghpair kez mi trosh,
Zor im tzerkov kordzetzi
Keeshernera yes koon chega,
Ardasoonkov luvatzi.
(repeat previous two lines)

Nayir neran yerek kooynov,
Nuviragan mer nushan,
Togh poghpoghi tushnamoo tem,
Togh meesht bandza Haiastan.
(repeat previous two lines)

Amenayn degh maha mi eh
Mart mee ankam bid merni,
Paytz yerani vor ir azki
Azadootyan ga tzohvi.
(repeat previous two lines)

Our Fatherland

Our fatherland, free and independent
That lived from century to century
His children are calling
Free independent Armenia.
(repeat previous two lines)

Here brother, for you a flag
That I made with my hands
Nights I didn't sleep
With tears I washed it.
(repeat previous two lines)

Look at it, three colors
It's our gifted symbol
Let it shine against the enemy
Let Armenia always be glorious.
(repeat previous two lines)

Everywhere death is the same
Everyone dies only once
But lucky is the one
Who is sacrificed for his nation.
(repeat previous two lines)

Yerevan: Did You Know This?

Yerevan, the ancient capital of Armenia, is one of the oldest cities in the world. It was founded nearly 2,800 years ago. Written records describing the city date back to 782 B.C., when King Argishti I built a fortress there. Artifacts from that time can be seen in the city's Erebuni Museum. In the 1930s, many of the city's older neighborhoods were demolished for public health reasons. They were rebuilt with heavy Soviet-style architecture using various colors of tufa and basalt, which are types of stone. Because of this, the city has few painted structures.

Yerevan is on the vast, dry Ararat Plain, which is about 3,280 feet (1,000 m) above sea level. The snow-crowned heights of Mount Ararat overlook the city.

Government buildings, major hotels, the Armenian History Museum, the State Museum of History, and the National Gallery of Art surround Republic Square (above) in the heart of Yerevan. Mesrop Mashtots Avenue is the main road through the city.

Yerevan has a population of about 1.2 million. More than 95 percent of its citizens are of Armenian heritage. Its average temperature from June to mid-September ranges from 71.6°F to 96.8°F (22°C to 36°C). In the winter, it ranges from 14°F to 23°F (−5° to −10°C).

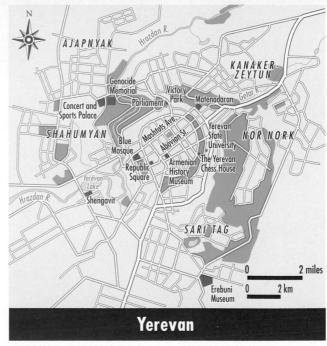

Yerevan

CHAPTER SIX

Armenia
Hard at Work

ARMENIA'S ECONOMY HAS BEEN SHAKEN BY SEVERAL major events that remain serious challenges to the country's ongoing financial stability and growth. However, the country's hardworking business leaders and laborers are trying hard to overcome these obstacles. Armenia is still recovering from the aftereffects of a devastating earthquake that struck in 1988. Homes, hospitals, churches, factories, and offices were badly damaged throughout the country. Another obstacle Armenia faced was the collapse of the Soviet Union, which was Armenia's major trading partner at the time. Lastly, the war between Azerbaijan and Nagorno-Karabakh resulted in an economic blockade and border closures with several of Armenia's neighbors. This turmoil severely affected the flow of goods and raw materials into and out of the country. In addition, political difficulties throughout the trans-Caucacus area, particularly in nearby Georgia, have caused economic problems for Armenia.

Armenia's own geography and climate also have presented difficulties. Its land-locked location, mountainous terrain, lack of fertile soil, and snowy winters each create problems. As Armenia deals with these issues, its economy remains largely a cash-only system. Smart shoppers always carry extra coins and small bills with them

Opposite: **Armenians take pride in their country and its economic growth. Here masons restore a stone wall.**

A vendor accepts cash payment from a customer at her small fruit stall.

because many stores cannot provide change for large denominations of money. Credit cards are accepted at only some businesses. There are few automatic teller machines in the country, and most of them are located in Yerevan.

Land of Plenty

Many Armenians rely on subsistence agriculture for their livelihood, which means they grow enough food to eat but have little extra. Most farmers work without modern equipment or knowledge of up-to-date techniques. Harvests can be bountiful, however, especially when irrigation is used to water the crops. More than 706,000 acres (286,000 ha) of fields are irrigated with water from eighty-three reservoirs.

This farmer harvests corn by hand with a scythe.

Grapes for wine making are plentiful in this vineyard.

Agriculture still holds an important place in Armenia's economy, despite the fact that the irrigation system needs repairing and updating. Getting the produce to food-processing plants and to city markets is often difficult because of bad roads and the lack of efficient transportation systems.

More than one-third of the population works on farms. Wheat, barley, wine grapes, apricots, pears, figs, nuts, peaches, olives, potatoes, and sugar beets are the main food crops. Grapes and other fruits are often made into brandy, which is popular on the international market. Thirty-five wineries are kept busy processing Armenian grapes. Cotton and tobacco are also grown.

A shepherd guides his flock.

Almost all farmers have cattle, sheep, fowl, and hogs grazing on their land, yet imports of butter, milk, and meat are still necessary to meet the country's needs. The annual value of the country's imports is larger than that of its exports. This is a situation that Armenia would like to change. It is better for the economy if the country is selling food and other products rather than buying them from foreign nations.

Today, there are 300,000 private farms, 1,600 cooperatives, and 150 large, state-operated farms and food-processing plants in Armenia. These replaced the 886 huge government-owned agricultural enterprises that existed under the Soviet regime. The Ministry of Agriculture and Food is in charge of putting into effect the government's agricultural policies.

Digging for Wealth

Armenia is gradually becoming better able to capitalize on its mineral deposits. It sells lead, gold, bauxite, zinc, and marble. Large deposits of iron ore, estimated at more than 550 million tons, have been found near Abovian and Hrazdan. Copper is smelted at factories in mining towns such as Kapan, Agarak, and Kadjaran. Gold has been found in Zod, Meghradzor, and Terterasar. The country also has more exotic materials, such as bentonite, a soft clay that is used as a fertilizer compound. Perlite is a glassy volcanic rock used in making concrete, as a filtration material in refining oil, and as a component in glass and ceramics. Zeolite is a mineral that helps purify water. Armenia also has rich stores of semiprecious stones that are used in creating jewelry and artwork. One of these stones is a volcanic glass called obsidian, which is treasured by craftspeople.

Resources

Cereals	Cotton	Au Gold
Vineyards	Pasture livestock	Cu Copper
		Mo Molybdenum

Armenia has natural stores of obsidian rock, which forms as the result of volcanic lava coming in contact with water.

What Armenia Grows, Makes, and Mines	
Agriculture	
Tea	472,000 metric tons
Olives	343,000 metric tons
Grapes	100,000 metric tons
Manufacturing	
Cement	304,238 tons
Paper products	23,656 tons
Copper-based alloys	18,477 tons
Mining	
Salt, unrefined	31,967 tons
Gypsum	14,330 tons
Copper-bearing ore	10,692 tons

To attract tourists, the country is building resorts near some of its more than twenty thousand natural springs. These resorts will capitalize on the healing properties of water containing mineral salts used to treat skin and other medical conditions. The water at Arzni and Sevan are among the most popular. Other waters are bottled for drinking.

In addition, the country's slowly expanding textile and chemical industries are bringing in much-needed money. Aluminum production has the potential for additional growth. Under Soviet rule, most of Armenia's industrial output was used to supply military goods for the Soviet army. After Armenia

Women sew clothes at a textile company in Yerevan.

gained independence, factories needed to be overhauled so they could manufacture more goods for the civilian market. That changeover is still underway.

When the Soviet economy collapsed, Armenia retained a skilled labor pool that continued to make intricate electronic equipment, including clocks and communication devices. Factories now produce laser systems, measuring instruments, radios, appliances, and spare parts for industrial machinery. The Ministry of Industry is responsible for nurturing this type of business. The ministry has encouraged firms making cable, wire, power transformers, generators, electric motors, elevators, and lamps. One firm makes stone-cutting tools. Another makes power grinders. Armenia also has a well-developed chemical industry that produces synthetics, paint, acids, vitamins, and medicinal drugs. Factories in Yerevan, Vanadzor, and Gyumri make cotton and woolen clothes, toys, furniture, dishes, shoes, and carpets that are sold throughout the former Soviet Union. It is hoped that new international markets can be developed for these products.

Armenia's workforce is diverse. Here, a woman works in a shoe factory.

Changing the System

When Armenia became independent, its government needed to quickly install major economic reforms. Under the old Soviet system, businesses were owned by the state. Centralized planners controlled production. This system was very inefficient. With freedom came the demand for private ownership of farms, factories, and utilities, such as electricity-generating plants and the telephone system. A new currency, the dram, replaced the Russian ruble.

Armenia's economic situation is not bleak. Many Armenians living abroad share their financial good luck with people in their homeland. They send money to relatives and even act as unofficial "financial ambassadors," encouraging investments from abroad. Foreign aid also brings in much-needed cash to start business projects and to expand others. Armenia has signed several trade deals with Russia and other former Soviet republics, as well as with Iran. It has set up trade associations to promote international business. The Chamber of Commerce and Industry helps the Ministry of Foreign Affairs attract foreign investments. The primary trading partners of Armenia are Georgia, Russia, Iran, and Turkmenistan.

Armenia is also making a strong showing in international trade events. CMTS '99, an industry exhibition in Toronto, Canada, helped by the Canadian-Armenian Business Council, resulted in eighteen trade agreements between businesses of both countries.

Because Armenia is landlocked, it depends on transport links through its neighboring countries for its imports and

Currency

The basic unit of Armenian money is the dram (AMD). One dram equals 100 luma. Dram notes are printed in denominations of AMD 20,000, 5,000, 1,000, 500, 200, 100, 50, 25, and 10. Coins are minted in denominations of 1 dram and 10, 20, and 50 luma. In May 2004, 1 U.S. dollar equaled 547.69 drams. The national currency was put into circulation on November 22, 1993. In 1997, a new set of banknotes were issued in honor of Armenian literary and artistic greats. They include bills honoring the noted composer Aram Khachaturian (50-dram); Dr. Victor Hampartsoumian, president of the Armenian Academy of Science (100-dram); architect A. Tamanyan (500-dram); writer Yeghishe Charents (1,000-dram); poet Hovhannes Toumanian (5,000-dram); and painter Martiros Sarian (20,000-dram).

Armenian money is very colorful. One side of the 10-dram note features the statue of David of Sasun (Sasuntsi Tavit), a mythical hero who represents virtue, faith, and courage. The building in the background is the central train station in Yerevan. On the reverse is Mount Ararat, which symbolizes the Armenian nation. The 25-dram note features an ancient wall with a sculpture of a lioness, along with Urartian hieroglyphs, a style of writing used in the first Armenian state, dating from the ninth century B.C. The 50-dram note shows the Museum of History on one side and the government building on the other. The seventh-century Cathedral of Zvartnots is highlighted on one side of the 100-dram note, with the Opera and Ballet House on the opposite side. The 200-dram note depicts the Church of Saint Hripsime, built in A.D. 618 in the city of Etchmiadzin. Flowers are shown on the reverse. The 500-dram note shows an ancient coin depicting the ruler Tigran the Great, with Mount Ararat in the background. An ancient manuscript and a feather are on the backside. A statue of Mesrop Mashtots, inventor of the Armenian alphabet, is on the front side of the 1,000-dram note, with the ruins of an ancient church on the back. For the 5,000-dram note, the pagan temple of Gurni is depicted on one side, and the head of the goddess Anahit is depicted on the other.

Railway transportation is
Armenia's prime source of
travel in and out of the
country.

exports. Politics is always a factor in getting into and out of Armenia. Until the Nagorno-Karabakh dispute is resolved, rail and road links through only Georgia and Iran are open. The Georgian city of Poti is the closest seaport and the major shipping outlet for Armenian goods. Both road and rail routes are gradually undergoing much-needed upgrading.

Businesses Connect with the World

Armenian businesspeople need to remain connected with the outside world. They often fly rather than depend on ground transportation. The country's two international airports are located at Yerevan and Gyumri. The airport at Erebuni is used exclusively by the air force. Armenian Airlines, which opened in 1993, operates passenger and freight flights between Yerevan and Amsterdam, Athens, Beirut, Delhi, Dubai,

Frankfurt, Istanbul, Kiev, Moscow, Paris, Sofia, and Tehran, among other destinations. British and Austrian airlines also provide service to Armenia.

The business sector keeps up with news from around Armenia and the world through Armenian national television and the country's many publications. Many read the *Armenian Reporter International*, which is an independent English-language weekly newspaper printed in New York. *Asbarez* is an Armenian online newspaper.

Armenia's publications are a valuable source of international information.

Despite all the challenges facing their country, Armenia's 1,630,000 laborers continue working to help make the economy stronger every year. Shoppers are seeing a wider variety

Armenians find a wide assortment of goods at this indoor market in Yerevan.

of goods available in stores as Armenia's economic health improves. They can find almost anything at the sprawling *Vernisaj* flea market in Yerevan. Hoping to attract customers, vendors shout and beckon from their stalls to show off their goods. During the week, they are usually open for business

from 9 A.M. to 5 P.M. and stay open longer in the warm summers. Shops also remain open on Saturday and Sunday.

Prices for automobiles depend on the type and model of vehicle. Russian-made cars cost between $3,000 and $6,000. A Western European auto might cost $10,000 or more. In the early 1990s, roadside vendors sold fuel from jars and barrels directly from their trucks, but it was not considered very high-quality fuel and was used only as a last resort. Today, brightly lit gas stations are plentiful in major cities.

Inexpensive means of transportation, such as buses and trains, are popular ways of getting around the country.

In Yerevan, trolley cars are a popular means of transportation.

Horse-drawn carts are often used in the countryside. There are 9,940 miles (15,998 km) of roads in Armenia, of which 4,702 miles (7,567 km) are motor-ways, 2,088 miles (3,361 km) are highways, and 2,613 miles (4,206 km) are secondary roads. The Kajaran truck route, linking Armenia with Iran, is the country's main international link, which was aided by the rebuilding of a bridge over the Araks River. Completed in December 1995, this improved road access helped increase the supply of consumer goods coming into Armenia.

In Armenia's countryside, many people use horse-drawn carts for hauling heavy loads.

Staying in Touch

By the early 2000s, there were 585,000 telephone lines in service in Armenia, and cellular telephones were coming into use. Public telephones located in post offices are used a great deal. ArmenTel is the Armenian telephone company. Private television broadcasting stations, cable networks, and Internet service providers are also increasing in number.

Armenians love staying in touch with family and friends around the world. There are numerous Web sites focusing on Armenian history, politics, religion, and art. There are many private sites, most with chat rooms, that allow users to talk with friends and relatives anywhere, anytime. This bonding keeps Armenians closely linked with their wider international culture.

The People of Armenia

THE ARMENIAN PEOPLE ARE OF INDO-EUROPEAN STOCK, which means they have physical and cultural ties both to the West and to the East. Today's Armenians are a blend of people of many ancient races who met, married, and had children in this mountainous crossroads. The Armenians most likely originated from a people called the Khaldians, who were related to the Hittites; the Phrygians; and the Cimmerians, who came into the region in the 700s B.C.

Some historians think the word *Armenian* may have come from the name of an ancient ruler, Aram, who controlled some of the area that makes up modern Armenia. The

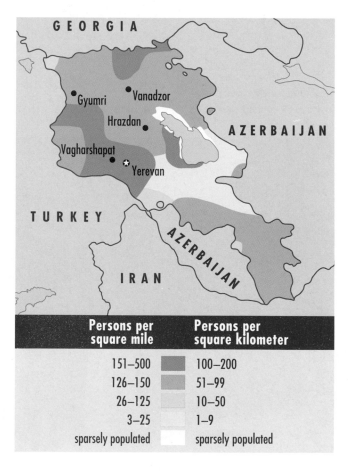

Persons per square mile	Persons per square kilometer
151–500	100–200
126–150	51–99
26–125	10–50
3–25	1–9
sparsely populated	sparsely populated

Population of Armenia's Ten Largest Cities (est. 2003)	
Yerevan	1,267,600
Vanadzor	147,400
Gyumri	125,300
Vagharshapat	66,300
Hrazdan	61,300
Abovian	59,300
Armavir	55,900
Kapan	43,900
Gavar	39,300
Artashat	34,700

father of a later king was named Erimena, which might also be a clue to the origin of the word.

For some researchers, Armenia represents a geographic area rather than a nation. Over the centuries, Assyrian, Greek, and other warriors marched through this much-fought-over region. Sometimes their reports talked about people living in a place called Arme.

It's All in the Numbers

Before the Ottomans massacred large numbers of Armenians in the late 1890s and early 1900s, there were probably more than 4 million Armenians living in their homeland. During the political turmoil that shook the country at that time, thousands of families fled to Syria, Romania, Canada, France, and Greece for safety. In the early 1990s, another 500,000 Armenians left their country to seek better living conditions elsewhere. As a result, there are more people claiming Armenian heritage living elsewhere than there are Armenians currently living in Armenia. An estimated 60 percent of the 8 million Armenians alive today live in sixty countries. More

Yerevan is a city that hosts just over 1 million people.

than 1 million each live in the United States and Russia. Cities with large populations of Armenians include Moscow, Paris, Beirut, Buenos Aires, and Los Angeles.

Even though the Armenians living in other countries have mostly been absorbed into their new homelands, they still love their language, religion, and customs. For instance, in Wisconsin, a picnic at Milwaukee's Saint John the Baptist Armenian Apostolic Church might feature lively Armenian folk music by John Paklaian and his band. Grandparents show their grandchildren the intricate steps of old dances, and everyone dines on traditional foods.

Young people make up over 20 percent of Armenia's national population.

Armenia's Young

In Armenia today, 22.2 percent of the population is composed of youngsters under the age of fourteen. In 2002, there were

Armenia's elderly are strong and vital members of society.

Most Armenians live in cities; others live in small towns and villages.

415,297 boys and 400,590 girls. The average life expectancy of Armenians is 66.4 years, with women often reaching their early seventies and men their early sixties. However, some Armenians who reside in the far reaches of the country stay active until they are in their nineties. They avoid the stress of city living, eat healthy foods, and keep exercising.

Seventy percent of the population lives in urban areas. One-third of these city dwellers live in Yerevan. In all of Armenia,

Ethnic Breakdown of National Population	
Armenian	93%
Azeri	3%
Russian	2%
Kurds and others (Jews, Greeks)	2%

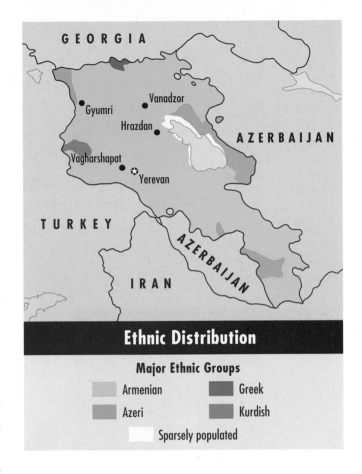

Ethnic Distribution

Major Ethnic Groups
- Armenian
- Greek
- Azeri
- Kurdish
- Sparsely populated

there are 27 cities, 31 towns, and 921 villages, with population densities ranging from 17 to 330 persons per square mile.

The Value of an Education

The Armenians are a highly literate people. About 99 percent of them can read and write. They value education highly and have about thirty institutions of higher learning. Armenia's first universities were founded in the tenth through the thirteenth centuries. Students have to pass very difficult tests to qualify for admission to the country's colleges and universities. These schools include architecture, business, agriculture, and teacher-training institutes; Yerevan State University; Yerevan State Medical University; several engineering schools; a fine-arts college; a state institute of theater and film; and campuses of the state academy of fine arts in Yerevan and Gyumri. The American University of Armenia is supported by benefactors in the Armenian-American community. In 2002, 26,000 students were attending college.

Among the forty private schools are the Moscow Contemporary Humanitarian Institute, the Yerevan branch of the Moscow Institute of Business and Politics, and the International Academy of Business. The Academy of Television and Radio is the first such school to be established in the countries that were part of the former Soviet Union. All of these schools accommodate about fourteen thousand students.

Children attend school between the ages of six and sixteen. First they attend primary school, and then high school, much

Armenian children attend school until they are sixteen.

like students do in the United States and Canada. Pupils study science, mathematics, history, economics, and social studies. When Armenia was a Soviet republic, some courses discussed the positive aspects of communism. After Armenia became an independent nation, those classes were quickly dropped from the curriculum.

The United States Department of State Bureau of Cultural and Educational Affairs is working closely with Armenian schools in what is called Project Harmony. Through the program, school administrators and teachers can visit schools in each other's countries. Participants learn to develop computer programs that tell about their schools.

Living Language

The Armenian language is similar to the Indo-European languages and is spoken by 96 percent of the people living in the country. There are two major dialects. A western version is spoken in the region closest to Turkey and by people living outside Armenia. An eastern, or Yerevan, version is the main dialect spoken within the country. During the Soviet era, Russian and Armenian were the official languages. Today, at least 90 percent of Armenians can still speak Russian. Only 2 percent of the people speak Russian as their first language if they are of

Common Armenian Words and Phrases

Barev	Hello (informal)
Barev dzez	Hello (formal)
Ts'tesutyun	Good-bye
Inch ka chika?	What's up?
Vonts es?	How are you? (informal)
Bari luis.	Good morning.
Bari yereko.	Good evening.
Kh'ntrem	Please
Sh'norhakal em	Thank you
ayo	Yes
Che	No
Anun't inch e?	What is your name?
Anun's . . . e	My name is . . .

A street sign displays the letters of the Armenian alphabet.

Russian heritage. Another 2 percent speak regional variations of Armenian and mixes of Armenian and the languages of neighboring nations. About 40 percent of the population speak Russian as a second language.

Armenian sounds something like Spanish, except the *h* is not silent and the *j* is pronounced like a hard *j* (as in the word Japan). A *kh* can either be pronounced *ch* as in *chutzpah*, or as the Scottish *ch*, as in *Loch*. *Jh* is pronounced like the *j* in *dijon* mustard. *A* sounds like *ah*. *E* sounds like the *e* in *let*. *I* sounds like the *i* in *fight*. *O* makes a long sound, as in the word *telephone*. *U* makes a sound like the *u* in *flue*.

Armenians often study English in schools. The language is understood by many office and government workers and by some shopkeepers in larger cities. Many young people speak English, too.

The Armenian language uses a special thirty-eight-letter alphabet derived from Greek and Syriac roots. The alphabet was devised in A.D. 406 by an Armenian monk named Mesrop Mashtots (left). He wanted to translate the Bible into the language of his congregation. He was helped by a Greek scribe named Rufinos.

A Nation of Saints and Churches

Armenians are very proud of their long religious heritage. In A.D. 301 they converted to Christianity. Their deeply rooted faith in Orthodox Christianity has remained intact and vibrant ever since. The Armenians' faith has not wavered despite persecution, war, earthquakes, and other catastrophes that have befallen them. As a result, much of the country's culture and art is focused around its religious beliefs. For instance, beautifully illuminated manuscripts were hand-painted centuries ago and preserved in Yerevan's Matenadaran,

Opposite: **A ninth-century church on Lake Sevan**

In Armenia, religion was often expressed through art. Illuminated manuscripts were regarded as treasures from God.

the Institute of Ancient Manuscripts. This museum houses more than seventeen thousand ancient writings that celebrate Armenia's spiritual history. It also catalogs works by important foreign philosophers and scholars, including Armenian translations of writings by Aristotle.

Well before Christianity arrived, Armenians were deeply spiritual. At first, they worshipped nature and the elements. Many of Armenia's mountains were considered sacred. Folklore described Mount Ararat as a creative, life-giving force. The poplar tree was special as well. Pagan Armenian priests, called *kourms*, were thought to tell the future and to communicate with their ancestors by listening to the rustling leaves. Everything to do with rivers, lakes, and rain was thought to be connected to the gods because water was essential for life. In addition, animals, the sun, the moon, and stars were thought to have holy positions.

Eventually, Armenians began to worship imaginary spirits and powerful heroes. The spirits were divided between good and evil and could take on many shapes. Among the good spirits were the *Haralez*, who looked like dogs. They brought dead soldiers back to life by licking their wounds. On the other hand, the *vishap* was an evil spirit who might appear like a huge dragon, a snake, or a fish. After the Armenians converted to Christianity, all these spirits became either angels or demons.

Adoption of Persian Gods

Because they lived in a crossroads nation, the Armenians were exposed to the ideas and legends of many cultures.

Saints Thaddeus (above left) and Bartholomew (above right) arrived in Armenia in A.D. 66 looking to convert pagans to Christianity.

Throughout the 400s B.C., Armenian spirituality was influenced by the customs of neighboring Persia. Many Armenians adopted the system of gods worshipped there. Among those deities, Aramazd was the father who created the sky and the earth. Anahit was his daughter and the goddess of fertility. She was a favorite of the ancient Armenians, who made gold statues in her honor. Ornate temples were built to remind the people that the gods were everywhere. Each of these structures had an altar called a *pakin* where offerings were made.

Most of the pagan temples, once famous throughout the ancient world, were destroyed when Armenia became Christian. Only one remains. The temple at Garni, dating from the first century A.D., is now a tourist attraction.

Armenia's pagan rulers had a great deal of contact with early missionaries, such as Saint Thaddeus and Saint Bartholomew, two of the first followers of Jesus Christ. These

Carpaccio's *The Martyrdom of 10,000 Christians on Mount Ararat* illustrates the legend of Roman soldiers converting to Christianity.

men came from Palestine around A.D. 66 to seek converts beyond the eastern rim of the Mediterranean Sea. When King Tiridates III was supposedly cured of a disease by a monk named Gregory the Illuminator (in Armenian, Krikor Lousavorich), he decided to accept Christianity. When the king converted, many Armenian nobles felt it was in their best political interest to follow his lead rather than lose their land and wealth.

There are many legends about that early Christian world, one that was terribly persecuted by the pagan Roman Empire. One legend tells the story of the ten thousand martyrs of Mount Ararat. According to the tale, nine thousand tough Roman soldiers converted to Christianity when they heard angelic voices as they were marching through Armenia. When the angry Roman emperor sent troops to fight them, newly sent troops were unable to kill the Christian group, even when they threw stones. That led one thousand more Roman soldiers to convert to Christianity. Finally, all ten thousand were crucified atop the mountain. A painting of this scene, created in the late fifteenth century by the Venetian artist Carpaccio, shows the attackers dressed as Ottoman troops. Relics, or sacred remains, of these martyrs are kept in French, Italian, and Spanish churches.

Walls of History

Archaeologists have located about forty thousand sites around Armenia that figure prominently in the country's long history.

Major Religions of Armenia

Armenian Orthodox	3,400,000
Armenian Catholic	180,000
Yezdizis	30,000
Pentecostal	28,000
Greek Orthodox	6,000
Baptist	2,000
Muslim	2,000
Jewish	500–1,000
Other (Baha'i, Hare Krishna, pagan)	300–500

The Blessed Khachkars

Khachkars are stone slabs carved with crosses and other religious symbols. They can be found all over Armenia. Most date from the early A.D. 800s to 1000. It is estimated that there are at least four thousand of these symbols, each with its own pattern. Monasteries used these images as tomb markers and as memorials to celebrate special events, such as victory in battle or the completion of a church. Now considered artwork, the khachkars were marks of faith and considered valuable spiritual protection against natural disasters.

Many have religious significance and date back more than a thousand years. Often, Christian churches were built on the ruins of pagan temples. The Armenians were very creative in building their churches, laying them out in the shape of a cross. This architectural style was eventually copied in Western European construction. The typical Armenian church also has a dome.

Armenian Christians remained under the powerful combined religious and political jurisdiction of the Byzantine Empire until the sixth century. The Armenian church then broke with the Byzantine belief in Jesus Christ's dual divine and human natures, in which Christ is considered to be both a man and a God. The Armenians support the idea that Christ has a single divine nature.

Since that split, which is called a schism, the Armenian church has remained close to other churches that believe the human and divine natures of Christ are closely linked. The Armenian church rejects the authority of the Roman Catholic pope and the doctrine of purgatory. Purgatory is a place where souls are said to go for temporary punishment before being admitted into heaven.

Armenia's religious capital is Etchmiadzin, just west of Yerevan. The city was also the political center of the country from about A.D. 184 to 340. It remains a holy place for Armenians because the cathedral there is the spiritual home of Garegin II Nersissian, the 132nd head of the Armenian Orthodox Church. Elected in 1999, he is called the Supreme Catholicos.

Importance of a National Church

The national church helped to maintain the Armenian culture by preserving the nation's written traditions. The church has always been a cultural focus for Armenians, no matter where they live.

Leading the Church

His Holiness Garegin II Nersissian was born in 1951 and entered the seminary in 1965. After graduation, he taught religious studies and became a priest in 1972. Garegin II continued his studies in Vienna,

Austria, and in Bonn, Germany. He quickly rose through the ranks of his church as a vicar general and became an archbishop in 1992. With this extensive background, the National Synod of the Armenian Church elected him as Supreme Catholicos on October 27, 1999.

Garegin II met with Roman Catholic pope John Paul II when the pope visited Armenia in 2001 to celebrate 1,700 years of Armenian Christianity. In addition to praying together, the two church leaders talked about the challenges facing the religious world in the twenty-first century. Garegin II has also reached out to leaders of other faiths to discuss spiritual issues.

For Armenians, their church provides stability and a spiritual home.

Over the generations, when Armenians did not have a country of their own, the church remained a stable political and spiritual hub.

The majority of Armenians recognize the religious authority of the Supreme Catholicos, and a minority follow the Catholicos of Cilicia. Both branches of the church were closely identified with the movement for national independence. There are other powerful figures in the Armenian church living in Jerusalem and Istanbul. Total church membership around the world hovers around 4 million, although the number of active religious practitioners is low.

Unlike clergy in some other religions, Armenian Orthodox priests can be married. A priest leads the congregation through the most important ritual in a church service, called *Soorp Patanak*, which means "holy sacrifice." This features the sacrament of Holy Eucharist, in which a small piece of unleavened bread is dipped into wine. During the liturgy, the bread and wine become transformed through faith into the body and blood of Jesus Christ. Another important part of the liturgy is the Kiss of Peace (*Voghchoin*, or "greetings"), which harkens back to early Christianity. The gesture symbolizes fellowship and submission to God.

The Armenian church celebrates numerous feasts and holy days that mark events in Christ's life, honor the Blessed Mother, and memorialize more than two hundred saints. Among the revered biblical characters, early martyrs, and church leaders is Patriarch Nicholas the Wonderful of Ephesus. He is considered to be the original gift-giving Saint Nicholas, whose image evolved into that of Santa Claus.

Armenians celebrate Christmas on January 6 rather than on December 25. Because the exact date of Christ's birth has never been established, the Armenians stick to the January date that was celebrated by all Christians until the fourth century A.D. The Roman Catholic Church switched the date the holiday was celebrated at that time to override a pagan celebration that took place in December. Some Armenians who follow an ancient calendar celebrate Christmas on January 18. Regardless of the date the holiday is celebrated, Armenians attend beautiful church services, sing carols, visit family, and prepare special meals on Christmas.

Easter is one of the most important religious holidays in the Armenian church. It celebrates the resurrection of Jesus Christ. Colorful liturgies involve the singing of marvelous Armenian hymns. Parents often paint eggshells as a traditional holiday gift to give to their children, symbolizing the rebirth of Jesus's spirit.

Major Armenian Religious Holidays

Christmas Eve	January 5
Christmas Day	January 6
Vartanantz	Thursday before Lent
Saint Sarkis	Nine weeks before Easter
Tyarnunkarach	February 14
Lent	March or April
Zatik (Easter)	March or April
Hambartsum	May or June
Vartavar	July
Assumption of Mary and Khaghoghorhunek	August

A Cradle of Art and Beauty

ARMENIA'S ARTS SCENE IS KNOWN WORLDWIDE FOR ITS depth of expression and beauty. The country's architecture, jewelry, painting, sculpture, needlework, and carpets are creative threads woven into an amazing mosaic of culture.

Armenia is a country of museums in which curators can safeguard centuries of marvelous artistic treasures. The National Gallery of Art in Yerevan contains artifacts dating back to the seventeenth century. It is also home to a huge collection of artistic works from Russia and European nations.

Other art facilities in the capital city highlight more contemporary work and include one featuring the vibrant paintings of landscape artist Martiros Sarian (1880–1972). Yerevan itself is also an open-air gallery. Dozens of statues by renowned Armenian sculptors, including Yervand Kochar and Levon Tokmadjian, dot the city's squares and parks.

Opposite: **An artist paints beautiful Lake Sevan.**

Painting by landscape artist Martiros Sarian

Sayat Nova, Armenia's Beloved Bard

Of all the noted poet/musicians in Armenia's history, the bard Sayat Nova remains the most revered. He was born in 1712 to a peasant family in what is now the nation of Georgia. Named Haroutiun Sayakian at birth, he earned the name Sayat Nova, or King of Songs, because of his musical skill.

Even as a boy, Nova was recognized for his talent.

He could speak Georgian, Persian, and Azerbaijani, as well as Armenian. This allowed him to perform far beyond his homeland, playing before kings and the common people. He was expelled from one court because he fell in love with the ruler's sister and spent the rest of his life as a wandering musician. He was killed in 1795 by Persian soldiers.

Many of the pieces depict the country's heroes, such as Vartan Mamikonian, a warrior who fought in defense of Christianity at the battle of Avarair in A.D. 451. Poets also get their due. The city contains statues of Sayat Nova (1712–1795) and Hovhannes Toumanian (1869–1923).

Young Artists

The Children's Art Gallery in the capital city was one of the first in the world to feature a permanent collection of works created by youngsters. The facility was founded in 1970 and quickly earned an international reputation for excellence. The museum also includes the National Center for Aesthetics, an art school for girls and boys between the ages of five and sixteen. Up to five thousand children are enrolled each year.

A book of Armenian fables, illustrated by children enrolled at the center, was underwritten by the World Bank. The students are also working on an Armenian Bible that incorporates their artwork. In 2002, a major exhibition of their art toured the United States, visiting New York, Chicago, and Milwaukee, cities in which many Armenians live.

Ancient Literary Lights

Armenia's literary tradition stretches back at least 1,500 years. Writers long ago wrote gripping sagas and exotic love poems describing their universe and its inhabitants in many wonderful ways. Modern Armenian writers now have Web pages devoted to their work, with essays, poems, and sample chapters posted online. They continue to describe their country and its history with emotion.

During the centuries when Armenia was ruled by outsiders, literature, poetry, and storytelling kept the people's heritage alive. Writing in Armenian was very important for preserving the cultural traditions of this ancient land. Yet authors often got into trouble with the authorities when demanding political liberty and cultural freedom. Yeghishe Charents, Gurgen Mahari, Zabel Esayan, and Vahan Totovents were either killed or exiled for their views during the early days of Soviet rule. Their story is told in *Writers of Disaster* by Marc Nichanian, an authority on Armenian literature who teaches at Columbia University in New York City.

The Armenian Research Center at the University of Michigan–Dearborn has a collection of translations of the works of many of the country's noted writers. Among them is Gostan Zarian (1885–1969), who was a prolific writer of short lyric poems, travel essays, criticism, and novels. Among his most famous books is *The Traveller and His Road* (1926–1928) and a narrative poem titled "The Bride of Tetrachoma" (1930).

An Armenian folk musician plays the kanun.

Music

Armenian music is one of the most unique forms in the Caucasus region, due to its traditional folk instruments that produce exotic sounds. The *duduk* is a reed device made of apricot wood that is shaped like a hollow pipe. The duduk's haunting sound has been heard in many movies, including *Gladiator* and the television series *Xena: Warrior Princess*. Other Armenian musical devices are the *kemanche*, a three-string, violin-type instrument; the *kanun*, a seventy-two-string lap harp; and the *tar*, a long-necked lute.

Aram Khachaturian (1903–1978), one of the most famous Armenian composers, often used these ancient instruments in his works. Born in Tiflis, Georgia, he became a student of folk songs and a specialist in Oriental music. Khachaturian wrote symphonies, choral works, and ballets that are still performed in the world's great concert halls.

Composer Aram Khachaturian

The Armenian Opera in Yerevan hosts many classical
events throughout the year, drawing international stars as well
as Armenian performers to its stage. The Yerevan State

Theatre of Song helps young musicians, such as Zaruhi Babayan, further their careers. Babayan's collection, titled *The Road to . . .*, won the Best Retro Album Award in the Fifth Annual Armenian Music Awards competition in 2002. She started singing in a jazz group at age ten and is a favorite of young Armenian music lovers. Rock musicians are also finding listeners. Yerevan's first nightclub opened in 1996, but it was not long before several others were in full swing, providing performance space for rising new Armenian musical acts.

Armenia encourages musicians from other countries to visit and perform in the nation, and just to relax there. Noted for its forested, rolling hills, Dilijan has long been popular with campers, hikers, and backpackers. But the region's scenery also inspires famous composers who visit a resort near the town. These personalities appreciate the quiet time that enables them to try out new arrangements. Visitors have included Russian composers Mstislav Rostropovich and Dimitri Shostakovich, and Benjamin Britten of England.

Theater Reaches Out

There are several regional theater companies in Armenia. Yerevan is the hub of stage activity. There are also many outreach programs to schools and hospitals. Each December, the Armenian Hamazgain Theater visits the juvenile and women's correctional facility in the town of Abovian to encourage interest in the arts. The Yerevan Institute of Cinema and Theater Art and other organizations help make such programs possible. Events are also staged for young

Tying the Knot

An Armenian wedding is always an excuse for a party. It is also an important cultural event. In the old days, a ceremony would be spread out over seven days. Relatives of the engaged couple visited back and forth between the homes of the bride and groom to "take the word," or promise to marry. This officially notified each family that the couple was going to marry. There were many blessings given by the local priest, and musicians performed at each stage of the event. Most weddings took place in the autumn, after the harvest, so there would be time for celebrations. Now, weddings are more streamlined and take place throughout the year.

Sometimes, the groom and his friends stage a mock fight at the home of his bride-to-be and pretend to steal her from her parents. Before the "warriors" arrive, a scout called the *aghves* (fox) steals a hen from the bride's chicken coop and then leads the wedding party back to the groom's house. Today, the "fox" usually arrives in a colorfully decorated car, but he still uses a live chicken to start the festivities.

Long ago, an elaborate wedding took place in the bride's home and was followed by a huge feast. Now, church weddings are popular. Yet even today, both the bride and the groom wear metal crowns, signifying that they are the "king" and "queen" of their new household. Gifts of shoes, copper trays, and handmade clothing are displayed to show the bride's wealth. This makes up her dowry, or items that she brings to the marriage.

The raising of the wedding tree is one of many important symbols that were part of an Armenian wedding. In ancient times, a real tree would be decorated with ribbons, fruit, and candy. Today, a metal tree is used more often. It represents the tree of life. The tree is the focal point around which everyone dances.

inmates as part of their celebration of the New Year and of Armenian Christmas on January 6.

Street performers who travel from town to town are highly respected in Armenia. The sight of tightrope walkers, called *pahlevan*, is a centuries-old notice that spring has arrived. One of the best young rope walkers is eight-year-old Hovhanness Armenakian. He learned the skill from his uncle, Hambardzum Umurshatian, and grandfather, Zhora Armenakian. Wearing baggy satin pants and a belt tightly wound around his waist, Armenakian can even ride a bicycle across the

Armenia's Stamps

Collectors around the world appreciate Armenia's wide selection of postage stamps that portray landscapes and commemorate important dates and personalities in the country's history. An Independence Day stamp features the tricolor flag of the republic. Another shows the pagan goddess Anahit. Stamps marking the 1,700th anniversary of the conversion of Armenians to Christianity and the fiftieth anniversary of the end of World War II are also popular. One series highlights the country's boxing, weightlifting, and gymnastics teams that competed at the 1992 Olympic Games in Barcelona.

tightrope. He is suspended high in the air without a safety net and accompanied by the exciting music of the *zurna* (flute) and *dhol* (drum). While the little boy performs, his uncle collects money from the crowd. Sometimes, the performers only earn the equivalent of two dollars a day for their efforts. Yet tightrope walking is a family tradition that young Armenakian is eager to continue.

Spain and Armenia (right) fight for the ball in the European soccer championships in October 2003.

A Nation of Athletes

Armenia's president, Robert Kocharian, is an avid swimmer who also loves playing basketball. He meets regularly with leaders of such sports organizations as Haghtanak (which means "victory") to discuss promoting athletics and a healthy lifestyle. Kocharian also loves hunting and often escapes from the rigors of his duties by taking long hikes. Following the president's lead, tour operators in Yerevan organize walking tours throughout Armenia's spectacular countryside.

Soccer is the national sport of Armenia, and fans of all ages cheer for their favorite players. Everyone was wildly excited when Sarkis Hovsepyan scored a goal against Norway in a qualifying match for the 2002 World Cup matches. Unfortunately, Norway won the game 4–1. But that lone

Many Armenian soccer players are members of the teams of other nations. Andranik Eskandarian was a defender for the national team of Iran in the 1978 World Cup in Argentina and then went on to play for the New York Cosmos. In 2002, his son Alecko (left) became a starter on the U.S. Under-23 National Team. Living with his family in New Jersey, the young Eskandarian was named the 2000 Gatorade National High School Boys Soccer Player of the Year. He earned the honor by scoring more than 150 goals in four years. Eskandarian attended the University of Virginia on a soccer scholarship and is preparing for the 2006 World Cup tournament in Germany. In 2003, he was the first pick in professional soccer's Super Draft, playing for DC United.

goal was enough to make Hovsepyan a hero in Armenia. It does not have to be a big international match to spark interest. Crowds always turn out for games between local clubs.

PYUNIC, an organization for disabled Armenians, has branches in Los Angeles, Chicago, Atlanta, and New York. The association helped several athletes with physical challenges to compete in the Sydney 2000 Paralymic Games.

Among them was Vyacheslav Oseyan, a twenty-three-year-old weight-lifter who become a paraplegic while fighting with the Armenian army in Karabakh.

Armenians have often done well at the Olympic Games. In 1952, gymnast Hrant Shahinian earned two gold and two silver medals for the skills he displayed in Helsinki, Finland.

Vanessa Rakedjian competes for Armenia in the Ladies' Slalom during the 2002 Olympic Winter Games.

Other athletes have won medals in boxing, track and field, diving, fencing, wrestling, and soccer. Armenia presented a strong team at the 2000 Summer Olympics, held in Sydney, Australia. On the squad were Hrachya Petikyan in the rifle-shooting competition, runner, Anna Nasilyan, and swimmers Yuliana Mikheeva and Dimitri Margaryan.

The Armenian weightlifting team did very well, capturing two bronze medals (third place). Arsen Melikyan earned his award in the 77 kilogram (kg) division. Ashot Danielyan captured a bronze in the over-105 kg division. Nineteen-year-old weightlifter Rudik Petrosyan broke the junior world record in the clean and jerk division by hoisting a total of 744 pounds (335 kg). He did not win a medal, however, because he was distracted during the finals when cellular telephones began ringing in the crowd. This threw off his concentration, making him misjudge the time he had left to lift the weight.

Whether using mental muscles to write poetry or physical muscles to toss around heavy weights, Armenians of all ages remain active and creative. Even playing chess is considered a sport. The Yerevan Chess House is named after Tigran Petrossian, the two-time world champion whose statue is near the building's front door. The father of current chess world champion Gary Kasparov is Armenian.

CHAPTER

TEN

Life in Yerevan

ZAVEN POGHOSYAN WAS HUNGRY. AS ALWAYS, ZABEL, HIS mother, had made a plate of *paklava* the night before. But she put aside only one piece of the sweet honey and nut dessert for Zaven to eat. The gooey snack was similar to Greek *baklava* and was Zaven's favorite treat. "I don't want you spoiling your appetite before supper. Besides, you have to leave some for Papa when he comes home from work," Zabel had warned before Zaven went to school. He knew his mother would count the number of squares that were left when she came home from work. She worked as a nurse at the Malatia Medical Center in

Opposite: **A woman stacks carrots in a market in Yerevan.**

Nurses at work in an Armenian hospital

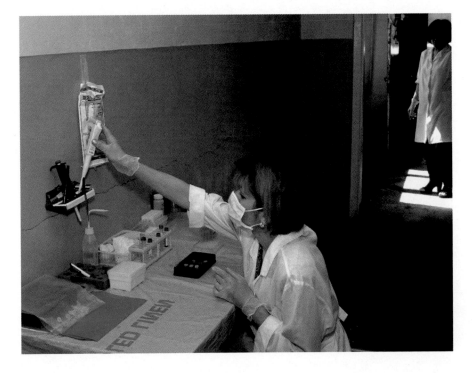

Yerevan, Armenia's capital city, and got home at approximately 6 P.M. His father, Ashghunji Poghosyan, owned his own auto repair shop and sometimes worked late. Mama always wanted Zaven to have gotten a good start on his studies and to have the dinner dishes set by the time she came in the front door. But he was to stay out of the food until dinner.

Zaven was twelve years old and tall for his age. He would be big, just like his father. Zaven's long legs helped him play soccer for the Atomics, his school team. A tournament was coming up next week, and Coach Marutyan was working the team very hard. Zaven and his teammates were really tired, and they often dragged themselves home from school. Eating an extra piece of paklava would have helped him perk up.

Apartment houses rise above the trees in residential Yerevan.

After all, he had scored three goals in practice and figured that he deserved a reward. But Mama's word was law.

Whenever Zaven scored a point while playing during a real match, he dedicated it to his father. Scoring a goal was also an excuse for the family to celebrate by eating an American-style hamburger at Mr. Pig, a restaurant at the corner of Abovian and Arami streets near Republic Square.

The Mother Armenia statue represents peace through strength for all Armenians.

Apartment Near Victory Park

Zaven and his parents lived in a small but comfortable apartment on a tree-lined side street near Victory Park on the north side of Yerevan. He walked to school every day, even in the winter. On his way, Zaven would always see the statue of Mother Armenia, which towered over the park from its vantage point on a high hill. In the old days, when Armenia was a Soviet republic, a likeness of Joseph Stalin stood in the same place. Stalin was a heavy-handed ruler of the former Soviet Union who arrested anyone who objected to his authority. After Stalin's death in 1953, the citizens of Yerevan tore down his statue. They then erected one honoring Mother Armenia. Everyone agreed that she looked a lot better than the scowling old dictator had.

Armenians enjoy a day of leisure at the park.

That was well before Zaven was born. So, of course, he didn't remember the celebration that occurred when Stalin's likeness disappeared. Now he enjoyed riding on the park's Ferris wheel and didn't think much about Armenia's past, except in history class. When he was young and Papa had to spend extra time at the garage, Mama often rented a boat to take a Saturday ride on the park's lagoon. On their pretend cruises, she brought along delicious homemade pocket bread called *kloz hatz* that was stuffed with vegetables and lamb chunks.

Because the boat oars were long, Zaven often had a hard time rowing. He and Mama laughed a lot as they went around in circles. They then beached the boat, and Mama spread out a blanket on the grass for their picnic. Mama liked talking about growing up in the city of Gyumri, Armenia's ancient trading center. Her father had operated a bakery there

Satisfying the Armenian Sweet Tooth

Many wonderful desserts are served at Armenian meals. Each family has its favorite sweet, and recipes are often handed down through several generations. One favorite is a delicious apricot yogurt cake that is full of walnuts and covered with an orange-honey syrup. Mint sprigs are placed on top for a colorful garnish. *Shakarishee* are wonderfully crunchable Armenian sugar cookies, which always taste good when eaten with fresh milk. *Halva* is a chewy, sesame-seed fudge made with brown sugar, vanilla, and *tahini*, which is made from ground sesame seeds. *Anoushabour* is a special Christmas pudding made with cinnamon, sugar, barley, almonds, hazelnuts, walnuts, and white raisins.

on Shahumian Street, so Mama had learned how to make excellent cakes and cookies. She told Zaven that when she was in high school, she had made a point of meeting Zaven's father at the outdoor market. His family owned a car-repair shop nearby. They would share popcorn and a soft drink and talk.

Mama had just married Zaven's father when a huge earthquake destroyed much of Gyumri in 1988. Thousands of people died, including two of Mama's cousins and her father. Jobs were scarce in the city because of all the damage, so the Poghosyan family moved to Yerevan to find employment.

Armenian National and Public Holidays

New Year	January 1 and 2
Motherhood and Beauty Day	April 7
Day of Memory (Armenian Genocide Day)	April 24
Peace Day	May 9
Statehood Restoration Day	May 28
Constitution Day	July 5
Independence Day	September 21
Earthquake Memorial Day	December 7

Armenian Church and Religious Festivals	
Sub Tzenund	January 6
Trndez	February 14
Lent	February or March
Tzaghkazard	March or April
The Blessing of the Grapes	August
Surp Khach	September
Navasart	Autumn

Mama's brother, David, left the city for the United States. He emigrated to Detroit, Michigan, where he opened a grocery store.

All Sorts of Jobs

Mama was able to get nursing jobs. Zaven's father had a hard time finding steady work even though he was a good car mechanic. The war with Azerbaijan over Nagorno-Karabakh and the economic blockade imposed on Armenia by neighboring Turkey meant that few businesses were hiring workers. So Ashghunji decided to join the army in order to get a steady paycheck.

Father Wounded in War

When Zaven was four years old, his father was wounded on the frontier and began to walk with a limp. He was a sergeant patrolling Armenia's border with Azerbaijan when his truck hit a land mine and he was injured. However, this injury did not slow Ashghunji down much after he left the military. Ashghunji had played the *zurna*, a flute-like instrument, and often performed at weddings and parties in the neighborhood whenever he had a holiday from the army. Since he was retired from the service, he had more time to play. He and Mama also loved dancing, and Ashghunji never let his old war wound slow him down. The zurna hung from a crimson ribbon on the living room wall next to his photograph.

Armenia's Traditional Clothing

Today, young Armenians wear Western-style clothes, complete with t-shirts, blue jeans, and tennis shoes, when they are just hanging out. Black leather jackets and pants, turtlenecks, or even short, slinky dresses are favored by girls when going to dance clubs. However, traditional clothing is often brought out of the closet for festivals and church celebrations. There are many regional differences in traditional clothing, the styles of which were influenced by those of the cultures surrounding Armenia.

Women were expected to conceal themselves with long dresses and veils. Even their hands were covered by the tips of their sleeves. White kerchiefs were worn by young women, and black head coverings by older women. In some areas, women wore aprons and mouth kerchiefs as well. For special events, beads and tiny bells were braided into a young girl's hair. Sometimes a girl had fifty braids, each with a separate decoration.

Men wore different styles of clothes in eastern and western Armenia. In the east, they would put on a cotton shirt, a wool jacket called a *chukha*, and a lambskin hat. In the west, the men wore a heavily embroidered cloth or lambskin jacket and a felt hat with a bandana tied around it. A man's hat symbolized his identity as an Armenian. In the old days, if he was unable to attend a meeting, the man could send his hat. If a man were insulted, it was said that "someone threw his hat on the ground."

Both men and women wore belts or sashes around their waists. They could be very simple or highly ornate, depending on the occasion. Shoes called *trekh* were made of large pieces of leather and were turned up at the toe, which made them look like the front of a boat. Fancy slippers with elaborate stitching were worn by women when they went to weddings or other important events. Shoes were popular subjects of love songs. In one, the man sings, "I'll earn a lot of gold/For my beloved/I'll buy a pair of shoes."

Delicate silver bracelets, head coverings, rings, and earrings complemented traditional clothing.

Everyone Plays Nardi

The most popular board game among Armenians of all ages is *nardi* or *tavloo* (backgammon). Originating in the Near East, the game can be traced back to at least 3000 B.C. It spread into Western Europe during the 1600s. Children love playing this game for two players. Nardi uses a board with counters that can be moved according to the numbers showing on tossed dice. Play consists of moving these counters up the board, on which are wedge-shaped points. The game moves ahead as the counters travel along the points to a player's home "table," where they are "borne off." The first player to bear off all of his or her counters wins the game. There are many other intricate rules that make for fast, fun action.

In school, Zaven wanted to do his best so his mother and father would be proud of him. His school recently had been-visited by two American teachers, who helped set up a computer program to link classrooms in Armenia and the United States. Zaven volunteered to work with some upper-level students to develop a Web page for their school. They could then correspond with schools across the United States. Students from other countries were also logging on to their site. It was exciting to get e-mails from Moscow, Durban, and San Diego. Sometimes the students sending the messages were of Armenian ancestry, and they had a lot of questions about life in modern Armenia. Zaven was really good surfing the Internet and determined that he might want to be an electronics engineer when he grew up. Zaven worked very hard on all his courses, knowing that he needed good grades and had to pass a tough exam to get into the university.

Finally, New Textbooks!

Zaven's school had also just received a shipment of new textbooks and other resources. Money to buy books came from UNICEF and the World Bank, which worked with the Armenian government. Zaven was glad that he and his classmates finally had some up-to-date things to read. When he first started school at the age of seven, there were not enough reading books to go around his classroom. Some of his textbooks were shabby leftovers from the Soviet era and were really out-of-date.

Zaven studied Armenian, Russian, and English four times a week. He studied mathematics six times a week, as well as biology, history, physical training, painting, and music. His six or seven classes each day lasted for forty minutes, with five-minute breaks between each. This gave the students the chance to run to their next classroom. Zaven and his buddies talked about soccer scores whenever they could.

Sometimes Zaven's class took a field trip to the children's puppet theater near Opera Square. Pretending to look at the

A girl pours a bucket of water over a passerby in Yerevan during the Vartavar festival.

swans in the concrete pool in the square, he and his buddies checked out the girls from other schools. From the theater, their teacher would lead them to the Children's Art Gallery of Armenia on the southwest corner of Abovian Street. That was always a fun place to visit, especially because Zaven enjoyed his painting class in school. After these trips, he sometimes thought he might prefer being an artist to being an engineer. He also dreamed of being like the bass guitarist Shavo Odadjion of System of a Down. Zaven and his pals loved the hard-driving sounds of the band, which is based in Los Angeles. The award-winning group consists of musicians from Armenia, Lebanon, and the United States. Zaven heard them perform on HYE-FM radio, which carries international music programs.

Soon it would be the holiday called Vartavar, which is held in July. Vartavar is the Feast of the Transfiguration of Jesus Christ. Zaven could hardly wait for the excitement to start. For several days around Vartavar, children are permitted to dump buckets of water on passersby. Nobody is allowed to complain. Even Mama didn't know how that tradition

started, but it was a lot of fun. Last year, Zaven threw some water on several soldiers. They just laughed and kept walking.

Zaven always had a lot to tell his mother and father as they ate their supper. It was a special time of the day for all of them. Maybe tonight they could have Armenian pizza, called *lakma-jun*, to celebrate his three soccer goals . . . and another piece of paklava, of course.

Family is important to all Armenians.

Timeline

Armenian History

The first permanent agricultural settlement is established in Armenia.	6000 B.C.
Romans take over Armenia.	190 B.C.
Tigran the Great occupies the Armenian throne.	95–55 B.C.
Tiridates III rules Armenia.	59 B.C.–A.D. 314
Christianity is adopted in Armenia.	301
Armenians are defeated by Persians in Battle of Avarair.	451
Arabs invade Armenia.	640
Seljuk Turks occupy Armenia.	1071
Mongols invade Armenia.	1240
Armenian territory is split between the Ottomans in the west and the Persians in the east.	1639
Russians begin moving into Armenia.	1760s

World History

2500 B.C.	Egyptians build the Pyramids and the Sphinx in Giza.
563 B.C.	The Buddha is born in India.
A.D. 313	The Roman emperor Constantine recognizes Christianity.
610	The Prophet Muhammad begins preaching a new religion called Islam.
1054	The Eastern (Orthodox) and Western (Roman) Churches break apart.
1066	William the Conqueror defeats the English in the Battle of Hastings.
1095	Pope Urban II proclaims the First Crusade.
1215	King John seals the Magna Carta.
1300s	The Renaissance begins in Italy.
1347	The Black Death sweeps through Europe.
1453	Ottoman Turks capture Constantinople, conquering the Byzantine Empire.
1492	Columbus arrives in North America.
1500s	The Reformation leads to the birth of Protestantism.
1776	The Declaration of Independence is signed.
1789	The French Revolution begins.

Armenian History

Russians occupy territory around Yerevan.	1828
Sultan Abdul Hamid II massacres Armenians.	1894–1896
Ottomans commit Armenian genocide.	1914–1918
Armenia declares independence.	1918
The Armenian Republic falls.	1920
The Transcaucasian Soviet Federated Socialist Republic is formed.	1922
Armenia becomes a separate Soviet republic.	1936
Armenia becomes independent; Levon Ter-Petrossian is elected president.	1991
The Republic of Armenia joins the United Nations.	1992
A cease-fire is signed in Nagorno-Karabakh.	1994
Robert Kocharyan is elected president of Armenia.	1998
Gunmen attack the National Assembly building and kill eight people; Garegin II Nersissian is elected 132nd Catholicos of Armenia.	1999

World History

1865	The American Civil War ends.
1914	World War I breaks out.
1917	The Bolshevik Revolution brings communism to Russia.
1929	Worldwide economic depression begins.
1939	World War II begins, following the German invasion of Poland.
1945	World War II ends.
1957	The Vietnam War starts.
1969	Humans land on the moon.
1975	The Vietnam War ends.
1979	Soviet Union invades Afghanistan.
1983	Drought and famine in Africa.
1989	The Berlin Wall is torn down, as communism crumbles in Eastern Europe.
1991	Soviet Union breaks into separate states.
1992	Bill Clinton is elected U.S. president.
2000	George W. Bush is elected U.S. president.
2001	Terrorists attack World Trade Towers, New York, and the Pentagon, Washington, D.C.

Fast Facts

Official name: Republic of Armenia

Capital: Yerevan

Official language: Armenian

Yerevan

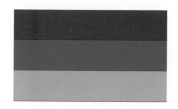

Armenia's flag

Mouflon

Year of founding:	1991
National anthem:	"Our Fatherland"
Government:	Federal republic
Head of government:	Prime minister
Chief of state:	President
Area of country:	11,505.8 square miles (29,800 sq km)
Bordering countries:	Georgia to the north; Iran to the south; Turkey to the west; Azerbaijan to the east.
Highest elevation:	Mount Aragats, 13,418 feet (4,090 m)
Lowest elevation:	Debed River, 1,312 feet (400 m) above sea level
Average temperatures:	July, 71.6°F to 78.8°F (22°C to 26°C); January, 26.6°F to 14°F (−5°C to −10°C)
Average precipitation:	8 inches (20 cm) to 31 inches (78 cm)
National population (2002):	3,330,099

Population of Armenia's five largest cities (est. 2003):

Yerevan	1,267,600
Vanadzor	147,400
Gyumri	125,300
Vagharshapat	66,300
Hrazdan	61,300

Genocide memorial

Famous landmarks: ► *Genocide Memorial*, Yerevan

► *Lake Sevan*

► *Matenadaran Manuscript Library*, Yerevan

► *Metsamor Museum and Archaeological Site*, Metsamor

► *Mount Aragats*

Industry: Agriculture holds an important place in the Armenian economy, with grapes and other fruits often being made into wine and brandy for exporting. Sheep, cattle, hogs, and chickens are raised for food. The country also mines lead, iron ore, copper gold, bauxite, and zinc, and quarries marble and rock for construction purposes. The textile and chemical industries have long been part of the nation's industrial base, with the production of electronic items growing in scope. More Armenian-made consumer goods, such as shoes, toys, furniture, and processed food items, are finding their way to shops.

Currency: The basic unit of Armenian money is the dram (AMD). A dram equals 100 luma. Dram notes are printed in denominations of AMD 20,000, 5,000, 1,000, 500, 200, 100, 50, 25, and 10. Coins are minted in denominations of 1 dram and 50 and 20 luma. In May 2004, 1 U.S. dollar equaled 547.69 drams.

Armenian currency

System of weights and measures: Metric

Literacy rate: 99 percent

Armenian youth

Aram Khachaturian

Common words and phrases:

Barev	Hello (informal)
Barev dzez	Hello (formal)
Ts'tesutyun	Good-bye
Inch ka chika?	What's up?
Vonts es?	How are you? (informal)
Bari luis.	Good morning.
Bari yereko.	Good evening.
Kh'ntrem	Please
Sh'norhakal em	Thank you
ayo	Yes
Che	No
Anun't inch e?	What is your name?
Anun's . . . e	My name is . . .

Famous Armenians:

Garegin II (1951–)
*The 132nd Supreme Catholicos
of the Armenian Orthodox Church*

Gregory the Illuminator (? –A.D. 326)
*Patron saint of the
Armenian Church*

Aram Khachaturian (1903–1978)
Composer

Sayat Nova (1712–1795)
Poet/musician

Martiros Sarian (1880–1972)
Landscape artist

Levon Ter-Petrossian (1945–)
*First president of the
Republic of Armenia*

Tiridates III (A.D. 238–314)
*Armenian king who
converted to Christianity*

Hovhannes Toumanian (1869–1923)
Poet

Gostan Zarian (1885–1969)
Author

To Find Out More

Books

▶ ed. *Armenia* (Then and Now).
Minneapolis, MN: Lerner
Publications Company, 1993.

▶ Kherdian, David. *The Road from
Home: The Story of an Armenian Girl.*
New York: Harper Trophy, 1995.

▶ Roberts, Elizabeth. *Georgia,
Armenia, and Azerbaijan* (Former
Soviet States). Brookfield, CT: The
Millbrook Press, 1992.

Web Sites

▶ **Tourism Information**
http://www.cilicia.com/armo5.html
*Tourism information, such as destina-
tions, images, guidebooks, essential
information, and resources.*

▶ **Country Index**
http://www.photius.com/wfb2000/
countries/armenia
*A listing of Web sites pertaining to
Armenia's economy, geography,
government, people, and more.*

▶ **Parseghian Records**
http://www.parseghianrecords.com
For Armenian compact discs and
recordings including all genres, such
as children's, classical, and contempo-
rary music.

▶ **Asbarez**
http://www.asbarez.com/
Daily news updates from Armenia and
Armenian communities around the
world.

Organizations and Embassies

▶ **Armenian Assembly of America**
122 C Street NW, Suite 350
Washington, DC 20008
202-393-3434

▶ **Embassy of the Republic of Armenia**
2225 R Street NW
Washington, DC 20008
202-319-1976

Index

Page numbers in *italics* indicate illustrations.

Meet the Author

Martin Hintz, author of Enchantment of the World *United States of America*, is a long-time travel writer and editor. He has written almost ninety books, including numerous volumes for Children's Press in the Enchantment of the World series, as well as many in the American the Beautiful series, which focuses on the United States.

Hintz has also written hundreds of magazine and newspaper articles for a wide variety of publications in the United States and overseas. Hintz is also publisher of *The Irish American Post*, an online news journal focusing on the Irish around the world. Hintz is director of the Mountjoy Writers Group, an international news syndicate. Keeping in touch with the rest of the writing world, Hintz is past president and chairman of the board of the Society of American Travel

Writers, North America's largest organization of professional travel journalists. He also belongs to the Society of Professional Journalists and the Committee to Protect Journalists, which supports and aids reporters and editors in trouble with their governments around the world.

To research Armenia, he interviewed many Armenians, visited Armenian festivals, read histories and political studies on the country, and checked the Web.

Photo Credits

Photographs © 2004:

A Perfect Exposure: 27, 28 (German Avagyan), 7 bottom, 12, 90, 120 (Cory Langley), 63, 93, 110 (Ruben Mangasaryan/Patker/APE), 96 (Rabatti-Domingie), 42;

AP/Wide World Photos: 61, 112, 113, 126;

Armen Housepian/www.ArmenStamp. com: 111;

Aurora & Quanta Productions/Erol Gurian/Laif: 99 bottom;

Bridgeman Art Library International Ltd., London/New York: 38 (Biblioteque Nationale, Paris), 123 bottom (Yale Center for British Art, Paul Mellon Collection);

Bruce Coleman Inc.: 24, 29 left (JC Carton), 32 top (Adrian P. Davies), 30, 131 (Eric Dragesco), 31 (Frank Krahmer);

Corbis Images: 95 right (Archivo Iconografico, S.A.), 50, 116, 132 top (Dave Bartruff), 41 top, 45, 47 bottom, 47 top (Bettmann), 95 left (Elio Ciol), 54 (Anna Clopet), 8, 19, 39, 106 (Dean Conger), 40 (Gianni Dagli Orti), 73 (Ric Ergenbright), back cover, cover, 6, 91, 92 (Charles & Josette Lenars), 58 (Alain Nogues), 33, 34 top (David A. Northcott), 69, 79 top, 118 (Jon Spaull), 43 (Stapleton Collection), 34 bottom (Roger Tidman), 68 bottom (David Turnley), 25, 75, 78, 100 (Peter Turnley), 114 (Tim De Waele/Isosport), 2, 26, 67, 72, 102 (Michael S. Yamashita);

Corbis Sygma: 51 (Bisson Bernard), 117 (Sivaslian Max), 79 bottom;

Landov, LLC: 56 (Ruben Mangasaryan/ EPA), 55 (Velichkin/EPA);

Panos Pictures: 66, 130 (Onnik Krikorian), 20 top, 20 bottom, 80, 81, 82, 88, 97 (JC Tordai);

Peter Arnold Inc./Hjalte Tin/Still Pictures: 127;

Photo Researchers, NY: 35 (Nigel Dennis), 32 bottom (Mandal Ranjit);

Sovfoto/Eastfoto: 16, 18, 119 (Novosti), 7 top, 37, 41 bottom, 46, 53, 60, 77, 99 top, 107, 108, 123 top, 132 bottom, 133 bottom (TASS);

Superstock, Inc.: 103 (Russian Museum, St. Petersburg), 10, 29 right;

The Image Works/Sean Ramsay: 71;

Tibor Bognar: 14;

TRIP Photo Library: 66 (Z Ananian), 22, 43, 67, 68 top, 68, 70, 74, 124, 133 top (V Kolpakov).

Maps by XNR Productions Inc.